隐形的爱
INVISIBLE LOVE
诞生-成长 BORN & GROWN UP

真真 Chen Chen

PARTRIDGE

| ISBN: | Softcover | 978-1-5437-5882-5 |
| | eBook | 978-1-5437-5883-2 |

To order additional copies of this book, contact
Toll Free +65 3165 7531 (Singapore)
Toll Free +60 3 3099 4412 (Malaysia)
orders.singapore@partridgepublishing.com

www.partridgepublishing.com/singapore

CONTENTS

ACKNOWLEDGEMENT

I offer my heartfelt gratitude to my husband, my three kids, our closed family members, my brothers and sisters in Christ, friends and relatives who lift me up with their unending support and prayers.

Special thanks to Aldrich Chieng & Matthew Wong of the cover design and coordination, Bliss &Co. make-up and photography, Vivien Liaw's hand sketched drawings, Rachel Yeong's help for English version proof reading, Lim Hui Hui and Ling Sie Ling for Chinese version proof reading.

Last but not least, thank God for His provision, peace and joy to accomplish my first book publication.

I WAS BORN

On one fine day in the year 1974, Little Chen was born in a government hospital in a small town on Borneo Island.

I still recall my mother's oft-repeated account of how the pregnant woman next to her bed was pushed into the labor operation room before I was born. When she and her newborn baby were pushed out, my mum got a shock because the baby boy's birthmark was spread all over the body, except for the buttocks, even the face was as green as "Bao Qingtian", the famous Chief Judge in ancient China.

Immediately afterwards, it was my mother's turn to deliver her baby. She had a smooth and natural birth. And when she saw that her baby girl had a birthmark too, her initial disappointment was turned to gratitude because Little Chen's green birthmark was just on her hip, unlike the baby boy next to her bed.

This birthmark accompanied me for almost twelve years, gradually fading out, and eventually disappeared restoring my pinky backside.

According to Chinese beliefs, a birthmark on the backside means the bearers are "born with a silver spoon in their mouth", and will have a worry-free life. My grandparents and parents testify that I was very easy to raise as a child, and rarely got sick. I started to walk when I was only ten months old. I am naturally left-handed, my eyes are naturally attractive, and I am an extrovert with good public speaking skills. I even succeeded in persuading my father to quit smoking before I even went to kindergarten - what a great feat for Little Chen.

In a blink of an eye, I turned five years old and could enroll in a kindergarten with a two-year syllabus. But we were not a wealthy family. The big three-generation family of my grandparents, my parents, my two siblings and myself, were staying under the same roof and my parents had a tight household budget that could not bear the financial burden of RM30 a month tuition fee. As young as I was, I told myself that I was smart enough to complete kindergarten in one year instead of two, so I finally entered kindergarten at six year old.

 1ST IN MY LIFE

When I turned six years old, I was happy because I could go to kindergarten. I was mature and also a fast learner. My academic performance was excellent. Because of my adorable appearance and moderate height, I was shortlisted by my teacher as one of the annual dance performers for the kindergarten.

I remember clearly that during the audition process, the teacher demonstrated a few dance steps among us who were shortlisted. Each child would then perform one by one to select the 12 most suitable dancers. This would be the first dance in my life, and it would also be my first time on stage. How could I give up easily? I remember clearly that I not only focused on observing the teacher's dance steps, when it was my turn to demonstrate, I did my very best to smile as my whole body flowed with the melody. I danced the dance steps as perfectly as I ever could.

"Chen Chen, you dance very well!"

"Just a moment, you are the last one in the back row and can't see you clearly. Come! Come! Please come to the front row ... Yes ... move forward to the fifth position ... Well ... Let me have a look ... move forward to the forth position ... um ... one more ... yes ... that's the second position in the front row ..." Indeed, the dance teacher noticed my desire and effort.

With a thankful heart, I appreciate that I was not only chosen during the audition, but the teacher also positioned me in the second position of the front row. My prayer answered, "Muddy Doll"- the first dance in my life was performed on stage successfully.

On the school's family day, the kindergarten held a children's obstacle race at the Primary school which is just two kilometers away from our kindergarten. I remember very clearly, I was childish and innocent but serious, I stayed focus and prayed that I will win.

"You did it, run to the destination ... Come on! RUN! RUN!!"

"Destination? What is destination? Where is the destination?!"

I looked to the left and right and finally saw my mother who was standing on my right. I ignored the voice about destination, and stayed focus and ran as fast as I can towards where my mother was standing and cheering for me.

"Child, the destination is not next to you, it's ahead of you!!! Please move on and rush towards your destination, the end there with a red ribbon...." My teacher's voice was loud and clear to me.

I thought to myself:

"Why should I rush towards that red ribbon?"

"I thought the red ribbon means it can't be surpassed!"

I'm puzzled, but no time to think twice, I did what I heard.

"Hurry up! Hurry up! Run! Run towards the red ribbon !!!" the audiences shouted.

Finally, in the "Make your own bead necklace" competition at the family day, I was not only the fastest, did not drop a single bead when joining them to form a necklace, but also within a millisecond, my brain processed fast to realize that I have to rush myself with a completed bead necklace towards the red ribbon or destination in order to complete and win the game.

That's how I won first place in the "Make your own bead necklace" competition.

Wow! It is also the first trophy I earned in my life. My little mind was filled with thanksgiving and gratitude. The glory of climbing up and stepping on the prize-giving stage as first was still vivid in my childhood memory. No doubt it nurtured a lot of confidence and good memories in my little mind. Indeed, it also shaped and molded my loyalty and positive character in my growing up process too.

HEAD OF CLASS CLEANLINESS

The following year, I set foot as a Primary One student in the Primary school where my kindergarten obstacle race was held. Finally, I could go to a school with such a large grass field and compound to sunbathe every day.

It is no wonder when I grew up, my face was covered with freckles, presumably the result of being exposed to too much sunlight when I was young.

I remember when I was in Primary One Yellow class, my keen attitude to learn, accompanied by my sparkling eyes, attracted the favor of the teacher. Instead of choosing me to be the deputy monitor of the class, I was nominated by the form teacher as head of class cleanliness. The reason was because our class came last for the past few weeks in the Weekly Class Cleanliness Competition. It was really disgraceful and shame on us. Teacher knew our class needed a breakthrough, an executor to work it out and make it happen.

"Yes! Sure, teacher has chosen you as the Head of the class cleanliness. I have confidence in you and you will certainly be

6

competent." Our form teacher came to my seat and affirmed me softly but clearly.

"Okay! Okay! I will definitely lead our Primary One Yellow class to be the champion in Weekly Class Cleanliness Competition soon." I assured my teacher confidently.

True enough I did not let everyone down! During the weekly assembly on Monday morning, the principal announced the champion of Primary One Weekly Class Cleanliness, it was none other than ... Primary One Yellow! The whole class stood up and applauded as I walked toward the stage steadily and cheerfully. I imagined that they were many journalists and reporters on the spot taking pictures of me as if I am the movie star walking on the red carpet.

Back in class, everyone came to my seat and thanked me for my leadership. My form teacher's affirmation and appreciation still lingers clearly in my ears until now. He said: "Teacher is never wrong to choose you as the Head of Class Cleanliness, I know that you will give the classroom's cleanliness a makeover. Thank you very much. Keep it up. Cheers!"

Indeed whenever there is a will, there is a way. I came up with a strategy. First, I to elected a trustworthy person to be in charge of every day's clean-up, and then pair him/her with a few of his or her close classmates. As for me, I was in charge for the cleaning on every Tuesday. With that, I divided the whole class into five teams to be in charge of Monday until Friday.

After class, all chairs were turned over and placed on top of the table. After floor cleaning, the chairs were put back into their original position. Then, we used a nylon string as a guide to straighten the table and chairs row by row from left to right, and from the front to back. In addition to my duty on Tuesday, I also assisted with other days of cleaning, mainly as a quality control supervisor, by ensuring that every day was clean and tidy, so that any time the teacher came to evaluate, our class was always in a perfect and clean condition.

I want to specially thank my neighborhood Aunt who picks me and other neighbourhood children up every day. Her old salon car couldn't carry everyone in one trip, so we had to be split up into two trips. I thank her for trusting me and allowing me to take the second trip request. Normally, Primary 1 and 2 children had to be transported back home in the first trip in view of safety concern and to avoid any unforeseen circumstance from happening at school.

With Aunt's special approval and favor, I could be the last one in my class to go home. This gave me the opportunity to carry out my task effectively as the Head of Class Cleanliness daily.

Every day I prayed (in my own way) of being on stage to receive the Weekly Primary One Class Cleanliness Champion. True enough, I did it! I am grateful to everyone who trusted and supported me, especially my form teacher, my classmates and my neighborhood Aunt.

TEACH ME PLEASE

I seem to have a positive and committed personality. If there was anything that was promised, I would do my very best to deliver. As I moved on to Primary 2, every night I did my revision by begging hard and crying out loud to my father to accompany me and assist me in doing revision.

In the past, getting a tutor or going to tuition centers was not popular, at least it not for our family that was living on a hand to mouth budget. We just couldn't afford such a luxurious spending. During my primary school time, apart from textbooks, there were no extra reference books or activity books. Homework was handwritten and copied from the blackboard.

Since we are a big family with three generations staying under one roof, my mother worked very hard for twelve hours a day in order to bring additional income to our big family. She worked in a shoe department as a sales person in the only shopping mall in our little town at that time. She returned home at ten o'clock at night, totally no time to accompany her children, not to mention reading or doing revision with her kids.

My father, who is also the head of the family, was just an ordinary government servant. Judging from the fact that my family couldn't make ends meet, my father enrolled himself as a part time life insurance agent and scheduled appointments every night to meet with different customers. Grandpa and grandma were illiterate, and my elder sister is two years older than me was overwhelmed with her own homework too. Either she had no time to teach me, or she just didn't bother to assist me in my study and revision.

Every night my dad still went out as usual, I couldn't stop crying. I begged him to stay and assist me in my homework that I couldn't do. I needed his help in checking my homework and to do revision prior to my examination on next day etc. Dad always turned me down and still proceeded with his daily appointments, hoping to close the deal. As usual, I was left behind and sat on the chair alone in the living room.

At this time, my little soul meditated on my own, turning grief and anger into strength, and determined that I must do well and not disappoint the elders' hard-earned money and expectations.

Therefore, I stopped crying and pleading. I listened and paid extra attention in the class. I boldly raised my hand to ask the teacher when I didn't understand his or her teaching. Since there were fifty-five children in a class, sometimes the teacher ran out of time to repeat longer explanations in class. I would go to teacher's office during recess time. I did my best to finish my homework at school while I could still remember and understood. My persistence, passion and never give up spirit finally came to harvest. My grades improved by leaps and bounds and I ranked number 9 in my class in Primary Two.

Finally, my vision of being ranked in the single-digits came true. I was so thankful and grateful.

WOW

When I was in Primary Four, my primary school had just started up a new extracurricular activity in sports-volleyball, which is only limited to Primary Four to Six for enrolment. My elder sister who was in Primary six signed up, so I just followed her.

Actually, there was only one reason for me to sign up. That is none other than to have fun outside my home as it was so boring at home after school. There was truly nothing to do besides studying and doing revision only. The TV program had nothing interesting on at that time. Cartoons were only shown at a certain time.

But a problem arise. The second trip of the aunt's transport pick up would drop my sister and I at almost 2 o'clock in the afternoon. How to get back to school at 2:30 in the afternoon?

"Little Chen, when class ends at 1:30 in the afternoon, we will ask Aunt to take us home in the first trip. Then, you and I only have 15 minutes to take a shower, have lunch and change to sportswear. After that, we have to walk from the end to the middle of Pisang Road West. We must arrive at classmate's house at 2:15pm, as her mother will leave home by 2:15pm to send her daughter who is my classmate and us back to school. This is the only way that you and I can reach school at 2:30pm, understand?"

My elder sister continued to instruct me: "If you want to follow me, you must hurry up, Understand? Don't delay! OK!"

"Okay! Okay! Sure! Sure!" I agreed delightfully.

Every Thursday, I was very disciplined and particularly quick and fast.

We reported for the first volleyball practice on time. Everyone followed the volleyball coach to do warm-ups. We practiced volley ball skills and techniques such as serving, hitting, smashing etc.

"Team, today we are going to select twelve inter-school volleyball representatives. If you are not being chosen, I hope you will continue to cheer for those representatives and keep up your attitude of continuous practice and never give up. If you are selected, you will have intensive training with me because inter-school competition will start two months from now. Clear? Everyone understand?" the coach said.

"Understand!" The team responded.

"Is that clear? Team?"

"Crystal Clear!" The team reaffirmed again.

"Well, team, we first select two representatives as serve masters from the team. Everyone will have ten minutes for practising. You will hear my whistle after 10 minutes. Then, everyone will line up and serve. Clear?" The coach issued the first instruction.

"Clear!" Everyone answered.

For me, being selected as an inter-school representative had never been my goal. It was purely for fun at the beginning, without having to stay at home and feeling bored. However, serving in volleyball was definitely a challenge for me, because I had never successfully sent the ball across the net to the opponent's end. Nevertheless, in order to obey the instructions of the coach and uphold the discipline of an athlete, I still bit the bullet and told myself to obey instruction and participate in the selection.

When it was my turn, I fully concentrated and brought out the spirit during my kindergarten "Make your own bead necklace" competition to serve the volleyball. "Pooh!"

"WOW! You finally did it!" There was an uproar from the team and everyone applauded.

Something strange happened in me, instead of being happy because I finally served the volley ball and passed over the net for the very first time, I was inexplicably depressed and ashamed. The team's uproar felt like sharp needles piercing my young heart.

I did not express this negative emotion at that time, but it was like a poisonous curse in my sports career. Since then, I began insulating myself from any ball game, and any sports that requires more than one player. Any sports or games that requires competition, I would stay away and stand alone.

At that time, a person had three serves. My first and only serve was successful, and the next two serves never went over the net as expected. Therefore, I was not selected. This was expected and not a surprise to me.

I still followed my sister and the inter-school representative team to every competition at different schools. I was not a representative, nor was I a backup player, I was just a self-nominated cheer leader. This was because my intention was to merely follow the team, wherever they go and just have fun.

When I was in Primary five, I quit volleyball practice as my sister went to middle school in that year. In fact, it also ended my desire and practice of any ball games or sports.

Unless the school PE lesson required us to play sports, I responded to sports like an "insulator".

PIANO LESSON

It's was the school holidays that I longed for, and to my surprise daddy did not schedule any appointment with any potential insurance client at night. So, after dinner around 7:30pm, my dad took me shopping at the largest shopping mall while waiting for my mother, who was a sales personnel at the shoe department to finish her duty around 9 o'clock.

Wow! When we were kids, we not only had our three meals at home daily, but also never dined in any restaurant or ate out. Even shopping was a luxury for my family too. Therefore, when my dad said let us go to the shopping mall one and a half hour earlier tonight, that became the most joyful moment beyond words I could ever express. That memory was so precious that would never be forgotten for a lifetime.

What was even happier was when I saw my mother, she even took time-off and brought me window shopping. I just realized that it was actually my mother's initiative to let my father bring me to the shopping mall slightly earlier. It was because there would be a piano demonstration and performance held during that weekend, and my mother wanted me to have an eye-opening experience about music.

I stood there as if I was rooted to the ground and indulged myself in the beautiful music of the big brothers and sisters who were playing elegantly and comfortably on the piano. At that moment, I felt like time had stopped and the entire world paused in front of me. I felt like I was floating on the melody, spreading my wings and conquering the world beneath me.

"My little sweetheart, time to leave, time to go back home after my long hours of work today." My mother's voice sound distant, was drowned by the sound and rhythm of the piano. I didn't respond to her. I just couldn't hear her.

"Little Chen! We are going home!" This time it was my dad's voice. I heard it, but I still didn't respond, and I was still hypnotized by the music.

"Little Chen! Let's go!" This time, my mother repeated out loud, without waiting for me to respond, she picked me up and dragged me away.

While I was being pulled away, I thought to myself "How could I, at the age of ten *in the Primary four,* ever win the fight with adult?" At that moment, my mind activated and triggered the magic weapon of "Crying Out Loud" together with reasoning and begging, hoping that my mother who was full of grace would hear and be moved.

"Mom, I want to learn to play the piano, please, I want to learn to play the piano. I really like it. I promise you that I will practise hard and do well ..." Repeatedly pleading like this, my mother eventually felt touched.

We went back to the platform, the piano performance that captivated me. A teacher in charge happened to observe my persistence and my mother's frustration, came forward immediately and invited us to sit down.

"Dear parents, we have discounts if registration were done this weekend and no registration fee is required. You are not required to rush into buying a piano. In addition, a piano book for beginners is given away for students who sign up this weekend! Oh, there are many benefits for children to learn piano. It helps the development of the left and right brains, and cultivate the temperament ..." The teacher delivered a really detailed explanation to my parents.

Standing by the side, I could sense the helplessness of my mother very well. With my family living on a tight budget, learning the piano was a luxury and burden for her. However, I was extremely interested (really really) in learning how to play the piano.

"Okay! We will pay 25 ringgit per month. We will sign her up for the beginners first piano class on next Saturday." Indeed it was a parent's heart and unconditional love for their children, that they would have to further tighten the family budget and become even more thrifty in order to give us the best.

I lived up to my parent's expectations. I got a Distinction in my Grade One piano examination, and was selected by the teacher to participate in the Year End choir performance. I was once again given the opportunity to perform on stage, it was a duet on stage. Some years later, I eventually completed Grade Eight of my music theory and piano qualifications with the Associated Board of the Royal Schools of Music (ABRSM).

Although after graduating from secondary school, I dreamt of furthering my studies in a Music Degree at the Royal School of Music, and pictured myself as an iconic and professional conductor of the symphony orchestra on the international stage. However, my academic qualification was neither excellent nor did I achieve outstanding grades. I was not talented enough in piano to apply for full scholarship or tuition fee waiver program and etc. Furthermore, education bank loan was a long-term commitment, so it was just a dream at night and life eventually carried on as usual.

LET IT GO

Back in fifth grade of elementary school, I was in Primary Five A class.

At that time, the National Elementary Chinese School Examination was conducted at Primary Five. If you get four As or above, you can apply to study directly in Form One in secondary school, and omit Primary Six of elementary school. The effect of this so-called "jump-class student" was to see how many pupils in the class would have the financial ability to go for extra tuition classes. Of course, the school teachers of various subjects gave extra past year questions and constant revision at school too.

I am extremely grateful to the teachers for their efforts. They not only taught us and ensured we understood, but also repeatedly reviewed and went through past years exam questions, to ensure that everyone's score was at the top of the list and able to achieve academic success. The dedication and responsible attitude of the teachers laid a good foundation and became a role model for me to live my life and influenced the way I treat others.

My class teachers made me feel very relief that it was nothing to be ashamed or embarrassed about if I was not able to go for extra tutoring.

Thank you, teachers. You taught well, I studied hard, did more revision, and I believed I could achieve the same result even without extra tutoring after school! This was my prayer at that time.

Finally, the results are out and ready for collection at school!

We rushed to school early in the morning. The teacher gave out the result slips one by one. Nervous and excited, I wanted to see it yet I was worried about the outcome. Sneak peek .. one A .. two As ... three As four As!! A total of four As and two Bs. I felt very satisfied. I qualified to be a "jump-class student"! Laa... Lalalala.

However, a weird thing happened at that time, I experienced an unknown struggle in my little heart. I worked very hard throughout the year, and got the desired results based on my persistence and teachers' guidance. But how come I felt a hesitation to apply to "jump-class"? Wasn't that what I longed for?

For some time, I was in self-denial that I was not one of the 5As student or a 6As student of the year. What if I was not be able to catch up with the junior freshman in secondary school? Then, I started feeling worried that what if my father's financial burden would increase again. I got curious about starting Form One and asked my classmates who had applied to "skip" Primary six and enroll into Form One at various desirable secondary schools. Another thought came to my mind, would I be bullied when I face the big brothers and sisters in middle school? I was worried that I might be too young, too naive and immature.

Alright! That's enough of the what-ifs! I had made my decision!

I decided not to apply for any secondary school. With that, I had no chance to be sad in case my application got rejected. Furthermore, I truly missed my teachers and classmates in primary school that I decided to spend another precious year with them in my Primary Six.

That's right! I've decided! I just didn't want to leave my classmates after five years of friendship, some even for six years of friendship (including the one year in kindergarten). I couldn't help leaving behind my beloved teachers who taught me to be somebody. I didn't want to miss taking Primary Six class photos and graduation photos too. I wanted to embrace every moment and I just didn't want to grow up so fast.

Once I decided to stay back, it was weird that it brought me peace and joy beyond description. I smiled during my own way of meditation. Feeling grateful for everything I had ahead of me, I did not want to miss them. I loved them.

1ST IN FORM 1

Thanks to our neighbor, who dedicated her entire career life to Chinese education and taught at the primary school for forty years with a passion to uphold and sustain Chinese education. It was she who came to our house several times and convinced my dad that his children must continue to study in Chinese school, and no matter how hard it is, the Chinese education must be pursued. This faith and legacy must be passed on. . .

True enough, my elder sister, myself, and my younger brother continued our studies in a Chinese Middle School.

In fact, this independent Chinese Middle School was about 20 kilometers away from our home. We must leave our home at 6:15 in the morning to wait for the school bus otherwise we would not be able to reach the school by 7 o'clock. By 1:30 p.m. after class, I rushed to the school gate because the school bus would drive away after ten minutes of waiting only. I often reached home between 2:30p.m to 2:40pm.

Breakfast was *Roti Kahwin* (Toasted Bread with butter and Kaya, sweet jam made of coconut milk and egg) ever since I went to kindergarten without fail. Lunch was taken at home around two to three o'clock in the late afternoon. By then, my stomach would often be rumbling and start to feel like having gastric. My daily pocket money was at most RM1 a day. So, with a limited budget like that I needed to be extremely thrifty. This was because there were three afternoons in a week, I had to stay back to buy lunch in order to attend two-days of extra tuition classes provided by our school for the National Examination (SRP for Form 3 and SPM for Form 5) in Malay language and another one day for extracurricular activities. This was mandatory requirement for every student.

I still remembered clearly that my pocket money was very limited, so I could only afford to have *Kolo Mee Kosong* (*Kosong* means plain noodles) as my lunch, because the additional meat and vegetables was simply beyond my budget.

Even with all the inconveniences of going back and forth to school, coupled with the improper meal times and insufficient lunches due to very limited pocket money, that still could not shake my strong desire to study. When I was in middle school, I was blessed with extraordinary concentration. A class of 58 students did not affect my concentration and distractions. Though I did not go to any tutor or any after school tuition class, my studies and knowledge ability to understand was equally competitive and aggressive. Reaching home late and stomach gastric problem would not stumble me from doing self-study and completing my homework. The most grateful thing was that although my memory was not photographic memory, somehow I had an extraordinary memory that could memorize a lot of knowledge and information quickly, accurately and retain for a long time.

I visualized that I could score and rank in first place, and I envisioned myself walking up the stage to receive the award.

True enough, my own way of prayer was answered. Not only did I achieve first place in my own class, but also the first place among all classes in Form One with a total average score of 90.17 %.

Thank you for the enlightenment of my neighbor who was the faithful primary school teacher, thanks to my parents for their financial and moral support, thanks to middle school teachers who were professional and dedicated in their teaching and coaching. I am so grateful that I have lived up to their expectations, topped of the list, and succeeded in my learning.

I MISS YOU, GRANDPA

Time flies. I spent five years in middle school and came to Senior Three (or also known as Form 6), the last year in my secondary school.

This year was also a very difficult year for our family, because Grandpa became extremely sick.

Grandpa was born in China before World War II. Around 1938, he decided to leave Guangdong Province in China with his uncle, traveled across the ocean, anchored and stayed put in Kuching to make a living. Grandpa's father died young when he was just three years old. He was the only child who was born in Shantou City, Guangdong Province in China. Because his family was so poor and living in poverty, Grandpa's first year of school life was at the age of seventeen years old. He studied Primary One at Chung Hua Primary School, Kuching as the eldest student among all the Primary One boys and girls. According to my grandfather, he only managed to attend elementary school for two years because he had to help his uncle to work and earn enough boat fare as soon as possible for his mother who was my great-grandmother to come over and reunite in Kuching.

My grandfather worked extremely hard throughout his entire life. He rented a stall at the corner and sold sweet potatoes, turnips, yams and many more at Old Market (commonly known as the wet market) in the early days. His income was meager, but he could still manage to feed his three sons and four daughters.

My grandparents stayed with us all the time, so I witnessed what it was like to have elderly people at home, it was like *"the home is having a treasure"*. I had countless good and precious memories with Grandpa.

Since childhood, my grandfather was my personal alarm clock, and it was him who woke me up every day. I had restricted my grandfather from stepping into my room to wake me up, or even knocking loudly on the door to frighten me early in the morning. Therefore, Grandpa sneaked his way out carefully and woke me up softly from the window for the past ten to eleven years.

Grandpa was also my faithful guard. Every morning, he took me and my siblings to the intersection to wait for the school bus. When we came back, we could see Grandpa holding an umbrella and waiting for us. He never miss a day, rain or shine, he dedicated himself to ensure our road safety.

I believed that Grandpa loved me the most, even though he treated his children and grandchildren equally and loved them just the same. Perhaps, it was because I was his most loyalty listener and had the interest of asking questions shamelessly. Grandpa not only told me stories about his childhood but kept repeating them again and again to me. He shared about the bitterness of starting his family, how the people suffered and survived through World War II and so on. Whenever I saw him closing his eyes and reminiscing about the past through his stories, I also felt like I had traveled back in time with him.

Personally I think that the most saddening and pitiful part of the story was that my grandfather dropped out of school after he was in Primary Two of elementary school. The fact that he worked and pushed himself to his physical limits just in order to raise enough money for my great-grandmother's boat fare to Kuching as soon as possible.

Grandfather's tough job at that time was to help the construction site by carrying large bricks from the dock to the site. Wage was paid according to the number of bricks successfully transferred from the dock to the construction site and had to be in good condition and original shape after several kilometers of walking distance.

In order to bring his mother to Kuching as soon as possible in the shortest time, he often overloaded himself and carried a few more bricks at the same time. Grandpa's logic was very simple. The journey was the same. Therefore, the only way to earn more was to carry more during the same journey. Furthermore, since the distance was already somewhat far sunrise and sunset would also limit the number of journey. There was no other way but to earn more by carrying more. While on the road, he was occasionally caught by his uncle who found him overloaded and pushed to his physical limit. His uncle ordered and instructed Grandpa to drop a few bricks by the side of the road. Grandpa was very rebellious and engaged in a fight with his uncle who was against him trying to earn more money. In the end, Grandpa had no choice but to obey unwillingly.

Grandpa paused and looked at me : "You see, Grandpa is not tall and severely hunched. It was due to carrying overloaded bricks that pressed on my spine during my puberty. Uncle's intention is for my good health and body's development. He believed carrying heavy weights would damage my fertility and cause me to be unable to multiply and reproduce, he worried I may end up with no offspring ..."

Grandpa was a workaholic. Although he retired, he could not rest for a single second. He actually had high blood pressure, but he never disclosed his physical condition. He still immersed himself in doing work in the backyard, clearing weeds was his favorite part of gardening.

One day, when Grandpa didn't wake me up, I went to his room and found that Grandpa had a lot of foam coming out from his left lip. He was unable to speak or sit up. "Dad! It's bad! Hurry up and call the ambulance ..." I shouted and rushed out of the room.

It turns out Grandpa had a severe stroke. His left side was paralyzed. While staying in the hospital for a month, my mother's father, my maternal grandfather was also admitted to the hospital due to geriatric disease, and their beds were facing each other, so that as family members we could take care of them at the same time side by side. *Ya*, it's a hard time for us, a tough memory.

When Grandpa's condition was stable, the doctor's advice was that nothing much could be done but to be discharged and to stay at home for good. The family's love was the best cure. Up till that incident, Grandpa was still very conscious, but after the severe stroke, he could not express himself via verbally, leaving only eye contact and his right side's body language.

I was in my final year, Senior Three Science Class. The results of my Unified Examination was the key criteria in determining the destiny of my future studies. I confessed that I was not contributing much in taking care of my grandpa, and I was guilty of not much filial piety. Instead, it was my turn to tell a story to my grandfather every day, and lend a hand once in a while to my grandma and parents in doing house chores.

In that same year, after spending a few months at home Grandpa didn't need to be taken care of anymore, he left the world peacefully one day in the late afternoon.

My personal alarm clock was gone, the doorman had died, and the story telling days was officially over. No longer could it be repeated by the original narrator, Grandpa.

I cried for a long time, but I could only imagine my grandfather in heaven, whom gave me the strength, to work for the best scores in my final year of secondary school, and to fulfill my dream of going abroad for further study. I miss you, Grandpa.

FORTUNE TELLER

The Middle School Unified Examination result was out!!! Wow! I got five As and four Bs. Although the result was not the ideal result that I prayed for, it was still acceptable.

Since I was from the Science stream, a class of forty-three students, almost everyone was busy applying overseas to various higher education institutions around the world after the results were released. In fact, before the examination, my classmates had actively participated in various educational exhibitions held occasionally at our secondary school premise.

During those times, studying abroad had many choices. Unified Examination was equivalent to A-level qualification that could serve as one of the direct entry requirements to various Universities abroad.

Some of my classmates were offered to study at higher education institutions as far as the United States and Canada. Some were offered universities in United Kingdom and Scotland, and of course a majority pursued their further studies in New Zealand and Australia, as that was nearer to Kuching. Some of us were planning to study in Taiwan. A couple of our other classmates continued studying A-levels in Malaysia, before furthering their bachelor's degree studies in foreign countries.

Everyone was so confident and eager in studying abroad, and each and everyone began to pave their way towards a bright and awesome future.

Although I had grown from a little girl to become a pretty young lady, I felt lost in the midst of such a major milestone in my life. Even when I imagine about my dream of going abroad to further my study, the efforts and actions for this dream to come true seemed so impossible. It was beyond my imagination and ability for the 18-year-old me.

Seeing classmates going abroad one by one, and the endless airport group photos taken to bid farewell and *bon voyage.* My dream turned into panic.

I could not act like the innocent and ignorant Little Chen in my Primary school. I could not repeat the tricks of crying and yelling to force my parents to send me abroad just like back when I wanted to register for piano class. At one time, I was patiently waiting for a good timing and good mood, to seek my father's opinion:

"Dad, may I go abroad to study after my Unified Examination?"

Dad paused for a long time and looked into my eyes and uttered finally, "Little Chen, dad can only afford to pay for you to graduate from secondary school, without any budget for you to go college."

I nodded and turned around, heading back to my room. As I walked, my tears fell without my control, and I dared not wipe it with my hands. I was afraid that my family members would notice my in disappointment.

Is the dream of studying abroad really unrealistic and fading away? Couldn't I find a way if dad doesn't have a budget? Since childhood, my own way of meditations worked powerfully, dreams always come true, how could it not be effective by the age of 18? It is impossible. The future path lies just ahead of me, wide and broad, prosperous and fruitful.

In my own way of meditation, I recalled my elder sister was studying at National Taiwan Normal University under the "Education Bond Program" of our Middle School. It meant her tuition fees and miscellaneous fees were fully subsidized, on condition that she would be bonded for five years after graduating to teach and serve in our Middle School. I had the interest to teach, a passion to be a teacher, and a desire to educate the next generation. This career sounds noble and satisfying. The most unfavorable fact was that my family did not have the budget for me to further my studies abroad. Therefore, this program may be the best and only way for my dream in studying abroad to come true.

Ok! I made up my mind and proceeded to Middle school to fill up the application form for studying overseas in Taiwan. I remembered very clearly that I filled out all the applicable universities and teacher's college in Taiwan. In the last column, my secondary teacher in charge suggested that I filled in the "National Taiwan Normal University, Division of Preparatory Program for Overseas Chinese Students" at LinKou campus. It was because if I could not receive any undergraduate offer from any university, at least I still had a chance to study abroad at the Preparatory Program, which was similar to a Foundations Program or A-Levels prior to undergraduate program. In fact, the teacher knew that I only had a "B grade" in my Chinese subject. According to her past experience, Mandarin is the main language used in all universities in Taiwan, it was unprecedented to receive undergraduate offer directly without going through Preparatory Program.

It was November when I submitted my application, whereby the first semester in Taiwan was scheduled every year in September. This was because the final year Unified Examinations was held in October that we missed the September enrolment in Taiwan. Therefore, from the application in November of this year to the first semester enrolment of September the next year, there was a long wait filled with frustration. A long wait, for the good news from the Taiwan Overseas Chinese Committee, filled with frustration because one by one my classmates had gone abroad whereas my future was still uncertain.

In order to not waste time waiting in frustration, I offered myself to be the home tutor for my neighbor's three children for all subjects. With that, I earned enough for myself to sit for my driving test and get my Class D driving license successfully in 3 months time. The rest of my time and savings was spent on a Test of English as a Foreign Language (TOEFL). I secretly registered for the TOEFL test, hoping that my English could meet the English entry level for admission to university in Western countries. That year, I also completed my Grade 8 piano Practical and Theory examination recognized by the Associated Board of the Royal Schools of Music (ABRSM).

When I was a kid, I wanted to further my study at the Royal School of Music in United Kingdom, specializing in Professional Conductor Course. After the TOEFL score was released, it was just a "pass" and did not meet the minimum entry level English requirements to study in the United Kingdom. Also, my Grade 8 piano results was only a "pass" too.

With the dream of studying in the UK shattered and my application for studying in Taiwan still pending and unknown, I was in the valley of my life. I decided to seek advice from a Fortune Teller together with my BFF (best friend forever) who was my classmate since we were in kindergarten and primary school.

Helplessly yet secretive was my way of doing things at that time, mainly to avoid my parents from feeling guilty of being unable to send their child to study abroad. At the same time, I had to actively find ways to fulfill my dream.

One fine afternoon, my BFF and I went to engage this old wise man, a fortune teller who was very famous in town for his prediction and *professionalism*. He was shocked and caught by surprise when he saw us.

"Why would these two young girls appear out of the blue in front of me?"

"What do you want from me? What can I do for you?"

We refused to leave.

In the end, our perseverance moved the old man, and he had no choice but to ask The Four Pillars of Destiny (known as "Ba-Zi" which means "eight characters" or "eight words" in Chinese). He flipped through his "fortune-telling dictionary" back and forth to try and predict our life. It took him the whole afternoon to write it down on one full piece of red paper. One person per page.

Surprisingly that afternoon, there were no other "customers" waiting in line or queuing after us, if not they would definitely curse the two of us as young idiots.

This fortune teller finally concluded that my life would be "prosperous and well," especially in my later years. He predicted that I would have many children and grandchildren. Anyway, it made me feel even more helpless at that time, because it was a drastic difference from my current situation at that moment. No matter, his positive prediction somehow comforted me with a kind of hope of looking forward to live on to a prosperous and well.

The wise old man gave me a new Chinese name - "姃瑑" a different character but same pronunciation as "Chen Chen", asking me to write and use it every day to improve my life through this new name. Very soon, it was revealed to my dad who scolded me for my silly nonsense attitude.

"Chen Chen is the name given by me to you since you were born. You have to trust yourself, believe in yourself and do your very best. Why go to a fortune teller? No hard work, no effort in action, do you think your life will prosper overnight?"

True enough, I didn't have the surprise of "prosperity and well-being" according to the fortune teller. The result of going to Taiwan to study abroad was released, and just like my teacher's recommendation, it was the last choice of the last column... "National Taiwan Normal University, Division of Preparatory Program for Overseas Chinese Students" at LinKou campus!

Well, things kind of settled down and I accepted the fact and fate with thankfulness. I appreciated the fact that I could pursue my dream to study abroad, even if it is not the country and program that I aimed for.

The following year, in the month of September, I went abroad to further my studies.

MY DESTINY

Thanks to all the "angpao" (known as red packet) and blessings of all kinds from friends and relatives, my mother said that she finally raised enough money for my one-way ticket, but she couldn't really give me any extra for my cost of living. I comforted my mother, saying it was totally fine with me, my elder sister had a part-time job there and she had some saving awaiting for me. "Mom, rest assured, I will be fine".

Finally, it was my turn to fly away from the airport, because it was September of the following year and Taiwan overseas students were the last group to go. Not many classmates were able to send me off and to take group photo together. However, there were eight or nine classmates on the same flight, and we felt accompanied and not alone.

We touched down safely and was given a warm welcome by the Sarawak Overseas Student Alumni in Taiwan who were there to pick us up. We settled down and spent the night in the designated dormitory. Before going to bed, everyone was asked to meet up in the hall, to attend a briefing followed by exchanging Ringgit Malaysia to Taiwan dollars.

"Hi Junior, did you give less? Why is there so little? Is this enough?"

The senior asked me out loud in front of a crowd of about two dozen of people. At that time, I wanted to find a hole to hide my head in. I really did not have extra Ringgit Malaysia. Indeed, that senior was straight forward, right to the point and revealing the fact that I only had so little and was truly not enough.

"Yes, Senior, you are right, because most of the Taiwanese dollars are with my sister."

This statement was originally used to assure my mother, I did not expect to repeat it again in front of a crowd in Taiwan. The difference this time was the same statement was used to console my fragile heart and to affirm myself that there was no regret in studying abroad. This was a white lie that gave me hope and strength to move on, not being defeated by external factor, such as the senior who was ignorant.

The next day, everyone departed early in the morning and went ahead to our respective university that we were offered. My elder sister also accompanied me. Since the budget was very limited, I only bought a quilt worth NT $ 290 (about RM 29). At night the temperature drops to seven or eight degrees Celsius in winter. I had to wear the only winter coat that I bought from the night market, which also cost NT $ 290 (about RM 29) to keep myself warm. Nevertheless, I managed to conquer the cold until my undergraduate final year. My suitcase of 20kg baggage weight carried hangers and detergent all the way from Kuching was still the same suitcase with 20kg after my graduating. Not overweight, nor underweight.

During Preparatory Program, I had two things to cheer for and to be grateful for. One was being elected as the President of the female dormitory and the other was the opportunity to work part-time at Administration Office. With that, I had enough income to cover my tuition fees including accommodation and meals.

I was studying in Engineering Section A. There were more than 200 overseas students from all over the world in Engineering Section. At the end of the first semester, my strenuous efforts brought me to rank 13th position among the 200. However, at the end of the second semester, my overall ranking dropped to the 31st position among the 200. This meant that I would be the 31st student in queue to choose my undergraduate program offered by any university within Engineering Section A.

Next morning, after having the in-house breakfast, I lined up according to my ranking. I felt butterflies in my stomach. It was uneasy for me because each student was given three minutes only to choose a desired undergraduate program out of 200 programs offered by various universities stated on the huge bulletin board, that hanged and covered the entire wall in front of us. Therefore, my undergraduate program's preference list had to be prepared in advance. Otherwise, I could not choose the desired and preferable program, my destiny was really a mess and I would be in a lost.

Ops! The 25th place picked my first choice. I could hear her conversation with the instructor because we just queued outside the classroom and leaned on the wall near to the windows above us. I kept wishing that rank number 26th to 30th would not pick my second choice. Otherwise, I would panic as I only listed down three choices on my palms, my sweaty palms.

When it was my turn, I selected my second choice without further thinking.

YES! My destiny was Industrial Engineering and Management.

I chose the undergraduate program from a national university, whose tuition fee was one-third of a private university only. Based on our senior's past experiences and sharings, you could make up for the tuition fees and cost of living by working part time. I chose a more interesting, less specialized engineering program, mainly to allow myself to work part time without neglecting my study.

PART TIME JOB

Apart from attending classes and obtaining my bachelor's degree, my life consisted of working at various part time jobs to earn my living expenses and tuition fees.

There were two semesters in a year, and each semester had approximately four months. The first semester started in September and the second semester started in February. Knowing that I chose to take a four-years bachelor's degree, majoring in Industrial Engineering and Management, I could only use whatever leisure time to work part-time. I earned enough only to cover for my daily essential expenses. However, I would work full-time during the winter and summer holidays in order to earn enough to settle tuition fees for two semesters. I was satisfied with my personal budgeting and part-time job strategy. All that remains was to carry on and work on it.

While I was contemplating on my part-time job plan, common sense told me to check out the restaurants within my campus premise. Working in a restaurant should be the best strategy knowing you could earn some pocket money and that certain meals would be provided too.

So, after seeking advice from my seniors who were overseas students from Malaysia, my first step was to head over to a bicycle parking area on the campus to find a used and abandoned bicycle that might be covered with thick dust yet unlocked. There was a common tradition practiced by the seniors who graduated, if they didn't intend to take their bicycle with them, they would just take the lock away and leave the bicycle in the parking area.

Literally, after two and a half months of summer holiday, used bicycles would naturally be covered by a thick layer of dust. It was a significant sign for juniors who were in need for them to identify and take those unclaimed and used bicycle. It was also a sign of heritage of care and kindness. A lovely culture practiced for decades.

I cleaned and rode the second-hand bicycle I picked from the parking area. I started looking for restaurants around the campus area with any job vacancy banners or notices of "Part-time Job".

The first restaurant, no "job vacancy" notice was found. I told myself it's better not to work there because it was a restaurant next to the male dormitory.

Moving myself to the second restaurant. However, no notice or banner were to be found on the ground floor. I walked myself up to the first floor, there was nothing that looked like a "job vacancy" notice. Well, I just could not give up. I told myself to approach the lady boss sitting at the cashier, knowing this restaurant was close to my dormitory, a very strategic location.

"Hi, Madam, do you need extra help to serve the food?"

"Are you available during lunch break? From 11 a.m. to 1 p.m. You can help to serve and scoop dishes for everyone who ordered and are queuing up for their packed lunch. After serving, you can choose one type of meat and two dishes of vegetables as your complimentary packed lunch. You can only take your lunch at your dorm, not here." The lady boss explained a lot.

"Good! Good! Yes, when can I start?" I answered without thinking.

"You can start tomorrow, Mondays to Fridays." The lady boss answered directly.

"Good! Good! See you tomorrow! Thank you, Madam." I was so grateful that my Monday to Friday lunches were settled.

I continued to ride on my "*iron horse*" to restaurants outside the campus, this time mainly looking for job opportunities around dinner time.

Walking and searching, I noticed one. I was so excited. Everything seemed smooth. A Taiwanese-style restaurant was looking for "work-study students." I walked in, and found the lady boss who happened to be there.

"Madam, do you still need work-study student?" I asked politely.

"Are you looking for work? It's mainly serving and cleaning, is it okay with you?" The lady boss replied.

"Yes! Yes! May I know what is the working time?

"Normally, we are pack with customers during dinner time, so please come to work at 5 pm. Our chef will cook dinner for everyone prior our peak dinner time. Typically, customers will start to arrive around 6 o'clock in the evening, and we will be busy until 9 o'clock. You may leave after tables and floors are cleaned. "The lady boss explained in detail.

"Ok! Ok! May I know when can I come to work?" I was overwhelmed and delightful, knowing free dinner would be served and the working time was just nice after my class. I boldly agreed.

"You can come to work starting tomorrow." The lady boss gave a sweet and simple answer.

"Okay! Okay! See you at five o'clock in the afternoon, thank you Madam." I was so excited. I kept nodding my head, waved at her while opening the door and danced away.

With that, my daily lunch and dinner were settled. On top of it, I still had income for breakfast and daily expenses.

Prior to the summer holiday, I managed to find a full-time job at the mini mart on the ground floor of the apartment located exactly next to our campus. My shift was from 4 pm to 12 am while the owner was taking the morning shift. Reason being the restaurant outside our campus would be closed down until further notice. The lady boss told us that she needed a break and rest as she had been in Food and Beverages business for almost 20 years, a life without weekend and holiday, and decided to close down until further notice. Thus, this became a reason that forced me to seek new job opportunities.

Because it was summer holiday, there were no classes to attend. I intended to make full use of my summer holiday. Knowing the fact that local students and most of the overseas students flew back to their hometown during the long summer holiday, so there would be a lot of job vacancies and tuition opportunities near the campus.

I managed to find two home-tutor jobs in the morning. One was a one-to-one home tutor to improve on an elementary school boy's mathematics just for the summer holiday. The other was teaching piano to an elementary school girl prior to her proper piano lesson that starts at her music school after summer.

In summary, my leisure time was basically from two to four o'clock in the afternoon only. Normally, I would take a break during these two precious hours by reading books or writing a letter and mailing it back to my hometown. After that I would take a shower and report for duty as a cashier at the mini mart by four o'clock.

These four years of college life would not be full of remarkable memories if I had not worked at so many part-time jobs.

As a part-time job, I was paid to have English conversation with a couple for two-hours a night, two nights a week. I am thankful to be invited to the couple's wedding dinner at the end of the summer. It was an eye-opening first time experience for me to attend a wedding dinner in Taiwan. I also experienced being a babysitter for a little girl still in kindergarten whose mothers was a single mother. She had a ten days overseas business trip in United States of America. My main duties were to be responsible for her meals, daily transportation routines and accompany her to sleep at night in her apartment. I worked part-time as a clerk for my professor keying in data and I even worked in the university's office as an administrator assistant of the Overseas Chinese Affairs Association located on campus. I even experienced playing the piano during some nights at the high-end restaurant in town.

No doubt these four years of college life were very tough and being self-sufficient was not easy for me. But, I definitely lived to the fullest with no regrets. These fruitful working experience laid a solid good mannered and positive working attitude for my full-time job in the future.

I studied abroad in Taiwan for almost five years, a year of preparatory program plus four years of undergraduate studies. After reviewing my diary and counting with my calculator, I only asked at most 5,000 Malaysian Ringgit from my parents for that five years. Basically, the one-way ticket for the first trip to Taiwan that cost about 2,000 Malaysia Ringgit plus the first semester tuition fees and some pocket money was worth around 3,000 Malaysia Ringgit. After that, the subsequent tuition fees and living expenses, including return air tickets were all from the hard work laboring of my part-time job.

9 VS 1

Females have an advantage when studying at a university majoring in science and engineering program. Especially the university I was in at that time, the ratio of male to female was 9 to 1. This was really an honor and privilege for all ladies on campus.

In Taiwan, it was very popular for social activities or singles mix party. Typically, the men in the university clubs or faculties would hold a fellowship party. Attractive flyers would be printed out and ladies from other faculties would be invited to participate through invitation, achieving the purpose of fellowship (socializing and getting to know one another) activities and seeking courtship or looking for potential life partner.

What I remember most, during one of the fellowship activities that is worth mentioning was "Fireflies Watch Night". First of all, men invited the ladies through one-on-one personal invitation. On the evening of the "Fireflies Watch Night", ladies were normally invited for a dinner. The humble or thrifty gentleman would order the most popular "take away" food such as deep fried crispy chicken chop and hot grass jelly before going to the dormitory to pick up the lady they had invited. 50cc scooter or 150cc motorbike was a norm and essential transport for everyone in campus.

At eight o'clock in the evening, school gates at the back were filled with vehicles, occupied by one gentleman and one lady respectively. When everyone arrived, they would just leave and head to the hill located at the back of our campus. Upon arrival at the destination, everyone turned off their lights.

WOW! The stars in the sky were shining crystal clear. It was the best time for gentlemen to lead the way in the night by holding the ladies' hand. After walking hand in hand, everyone reached their best spot for watching fireflies. A big piece of land surrounded by bushes. I was overwhelmed by the sight of bushes all covered with twinkling fireflies and the sky that was filled with bright with shining stars, like a fine piece of art.

I did have a couple of romantic true stories of being "chased after" by the guys in campus. Here I would like to share some precious moments and impressive stories of the of "9 to 1" male to female ratio.

Knowing my time was fully occupied from attending classes and working at part-time jobs. I actually had no time left for myself to fall in love with someone simply because I just no free time to be "chased after" and courtship with one another unless the guy was so dedicated in the relationship and persistence to press on.

I remembered during the first winter holiday in Taiwan, instead of going back home to my hometown in Borneo Island to celebrate Chinese New Year, I went to a bakery shop with another female overseas student to work full time. There was a guy who came to visit us every day, helped us to pull down the roller shutters every night, something that was hard for us to reach and tough to pull down. He walked us back to the dormitory, and later came out again for supper and chatting sessions.

There was another guy from overseas, who was a top student from a different engineering faculty. I truly appreciate his call one afternoon because I had collapsed and fainted. I found myself on the ground at my dormitory due to severe gastric pain caused by skipping breakfast and lunch on that day. My room-mate answered the call and requested for help to send me to hospital. As fast as you can imagine, he appeared at our door step with his motorbike ready at the lobby. Indeed I could not remember how I was carried and put on his motorbike, but on the way to the hospital, I could hear him clearly.

"Hold on to me tightly, we are almost there!"

When I opened my eyes, the first person I saw next to my hospital bed was the top student. The porridge at the side table was a "Take Away" ordered by him too. His selfless and dedicated care that day was one that I treasured forever in my lifetime. I saved even more money and allocated a big portion of my daily expenses to budget up so that I could visit his hometown in Macau. My sincere gesture to thank him who was my life saver at that moment. Well, no "love chemistry" generated from me as I was just too homesick and against long distance relationship and cross cultural marriage. So, everything went back to normal and life went on as normal.

There was a male senior, who knew that I would jog to keep fit at the Sport Stadium on certain nights. He then would also go there and bump into me as if "what a coincidence that we meet again". He knew that I had gastric problem, therefore he would occasionally buy me supper. Ya, we met and chat but it seemed like I was cold-hearted. The truth was I wanted to remain single and life still went on as normal.

During my final year, my class organized a group tour travelling around Taiwan, also named as Formosa Island. Among us, a male classmate, carried back a large bag of sand from the beach, and stayed up all night to sift through the sand for the "star" sand. Nobody knew what his intention was, or who would be the Princess in his mind to receive the star-shaped sand. Everyone was exhausted but felt happy after this 7 days 6 nights group tour. When we return to campus, shortly after settling myself at the dormitory, I received a call from this male classmate who carried a large bag of sand.

"Hello, is that Chen Chen? Can I invite you for a meal tonight?" The guy expressed politely but sincerely.

"Sure, may I know what time is it? Wait for you at the dormitory lobby, right?"

"Ya, half past six in the evening. Yes, see you at the dormitory lobby then. Bye!" He hanged up the phone with lots of joy.

Actually, a week of hard work, making this little tiny bottle of natural star-shaped sand was meant to be given it to me.

"Ops, are you going to give it to me? But.. I will be flying back to Kuching next week. For you, please continue with your master's degree. Please don't let me be the stumbling block of your great future." I expressed it straightforwardly.

"It's okay, please accept and keep it. This is my act of love for you and my sincere confession. I hope we still keep in touch after you go back to your home town. In case you miss me, you are most welcome to visit me in Taiwan any time, or any day. Your accommodation and meals shall be well taken care of by me... as long as you are willing to come back to Taiwan..." The guy said implicitly.

"Sure, keep in touch. Thank you for your natural star-shaped star. I promise I will safeguard it with me forever." I really kept my promise. I said it and I meant it. Even though I moved a few times after coming back to Kuching for good, I still kept this bottle with me. The only thing I didn't do was I never return to his home in Taiwan despite accommodation and meals would be fully sponsored. Ya, we did not develop the friendship further to another stage.

The next day, another male classmate also invited me for dinner to bid farewell for me, knowing I was going back to Kuching in the next few days.

"Chen Chen, are you in a hurry to go home after dinner?" He asked

"Em..well...I just have one luggage and it's packed." I answered.

"I know you will be back to Kuching the day after tomorrow, may I offer you a ride to airport?" He sincerely expressed his love by offering the ride.

"It's okay. I have confirmed with the owner of the mini mart which I used to work as a cashier. He will take me to the airport. Thank you!"

"No worries, we shall meet again. I will definitely come back to attend your undergraduate convocation." I answered with conviction.

"In that case anyway... the night is still young, please allow me to do my very best as a host, and take you to tour around the city, as a way of saying goodbye to Hsinchu City. Okay?"

"Okay! Great! Thank you in advance. A pleasure to be your guest."

In fact, he intended to take me back to his home in Hsinchu City as a guest. Apart from introducing me to his mother, he also introduced his home sweet home to me. He sincerely expressed that everything was in place at his home and except a hostess.

Suddenly, an ecstatic feeling of wanting to be loved made me indulge in the illusion of happiness and love fantasy for quite awhile until my logical thinking kicked in and "woke" me up. A firm word slipped out from my lip: "Uh ... ha ha ha ha ... I'm going back to Kuching ... I wish you success in your master degree. Wish you all the best."

One after another, countless love stories just came to a stop after I came back to Kuching. Such was the "9 to 1" precious memories that would be locked in my heart forever.

STOP BANKING IN

The dormitory in the campus was a room for four people, with bunk beds on each side. Thankfully, in the third and fourth year of my undergraduate study, one of my roommates was also my classmate. Thanks to the school for such a fortunate arrangement, I appreciated the warmth of my roommate for her love and care. We looked out for each other.

During one of the summer holidays, I thought of an absolutely foolproof arrangement to earn enough money for the next two semesters tuition fees by working throughout the entire two to three months summer break. However, because of the precious "9 vs 1" love experiences, I promised that life-saver overseas top student that I would thank him and visit Macau in person. This sudden promise caused me to over budget and unable to make enough for the following years, semester of tuition fees prior to class starting.

In my third year, my sister also graduated and returned to Kuching to serve her education bond as a teacher in our former Middle School. My younger brother had just come to Taiwan for the first year of his undergraduate degree. Therefore, I couldn't ask my family for any extra money. Moreover, I never asked my family for any living expenses or tuition fees ever since I came to Taiwan.

"Ting, can you help to pay my tuition fees for this semester first? I will divide it into three installments and transfer the cash to your bank account every time I receive my wage at the end of the month. Is it okay?" Finally, I asked for financial assistance from my roommate cum classmate.

"No problem, don't be so shy! You are occupied by your part-time job on top of your usual studies, it's tough enough. I will help you to settle this semester tuition fees first. Small matter, yeah! My dad gives me a lot of pocket money every month, and I don't have much to spend. ". Ting generously told me not to return her!

"No! No! It's my principle to borrow and repay. A principle that I believe in. Furthermore, we meet every day. I'm embarrassed if I owe you!" I responded.

"Well! Okay! I really don't mind, but as your wish!"

"I will transfer the exact amount to the designated bank account of the Account Department now, and state your student ID. At the end of the month, you can transfer anytime at your convenience. Don't worry! Really don't worry." Ting said politely.

"Okay! Okay! Thank you. It's nice to have you ..." I said gratefully.

In a glimpse, it was the last day of the month. I kept my promise and transferred one third of the promised amount to Ting's bank account. During the subsequent weekends when I was not required to work in the campus restaurant, a loaf of taro bread was my breakfast, lunch and dinner. Two slices for breakfast, four slices for lunch and the last four slices for dinner. Sometimes I just had cookies.

Anyway, I ended up with undernourishment. I experienced dizziness every time I stood up from a squat. It felt like I just went on a roller coaster or spinning wheel.

However, in order to adhere to my principle of being a trustworthy person, I'd rather choose to keep my promise and remained poor at that time. At the end of the second month, I transferred the second one-third of my balance to Ting's bank account as usual. I was confident in my heart, because I could resume my normal diet after next month when I settled the remaining one third of the balance.

"Chen ... My dad has something to tell you ..." Ting said and gave me the dormitory phone extension.

"What? Is your dad going to scold me for borrowing money from you and dragging on so long to pay back? !!!!" I turned pale and felt guilty.

"No! No! I told him, he insist on explaining to you. Okay, okay, you just answer the phone! Please..." Ting begged me to cooperate with her.

My hands were shaking and my mind went blank. I remembered during one of our chats before bedtime, Ting once mentioned that in her family, her father who was a soldier. If he said "YES", no one dared to say "No". She also mentioned that her father did not allow her to do part-time job during her studies, the purpose was to keep her focus on her studies, completing undergraduate and proceed to a master degree.

"Hello, Uncle ... I'm Chen Chen ... Ting's roommate ... Is there anything that you're looking for me?" I stammered softly.

"Chen, Uncle noticed two cash transfer banked into Ting's bank account. Ting clarified that it was not earned through any part-time job, neither any scholarship award. It was the bank transfer transaction from you to her..." came a loud and steady voice from the other end of the phone conversation.

"I'm sorry, Uncle, I asked Ting to help me pay for my tuition fee first, but I promised her to pay in three months, and next month will be last month. I'm sorry ... Uncle ... I'm sorry ..." I apologized, interrupting the conversation while tears rolled down my chin.

"Chen, Uncle does not mean that. Uncle calls because Uncle wants to ask you to stop banking in."

"Chen, Uncle understands that you are an overseas Chinese student who has been working very hard at part time jobs in order to study abroad. Please stop banking in. You don't need to bank in anymore next month. Uncle called you today to tell you that you don't need to bank in again. Okay?" Uncle explained the intention of the call in one breath.

"Thank you Uncle! Thank you Uncle! I'm sorry I misunderstood your intention. Thank you Uncle ..." At that time, no words could express my gratitude and thanks.

Indeed, this dream to study abroad, would not come true without the countless help and precious love from people around me along the way. When can I pay back to each and everyone of them?

Another classmate of mine was also one of my great help. He lend me his 50cc scooter to make my travels faster and more convenient to move around. That way at least I could travel further outside campus to look for even better part-time job opportunity. Although he said he wanted to upgrade to a 150cc motorbike, he could actually sell this 50cc and buy a new one with less deposit to settle. However, he just said he was in no hurry and that I could use it freely. I was so grateful that no major breakdown or parts that needed replacement apart from regular vehicle servicing during this period.

I remembered when I returned the motorbike to him after my final year, he just sold it. His sincere help without asking for any pay back was something I really appreciate from the bottom of my heart forever.

FINAL YEAR

Finally, it was the last semester of my final year, despite the hard work of studying and working at part-time jobs.

I remember very clearly that there were 52 undergraduates in my class; 50 Taiwanese plus two overseas students, one from Macau and the other was myself from Kuching, Sarawak, Malaysia.

On top of being occupied in planning a group tour for our class, our class committee also discussed who would be the representative of our class to go on stage to receive the certificates during our convocation ceremony. This was because our university had about two thousand undergraduates and postgraduates students, including bachelor's degree students, master's degree students and doctorate students who had completed their studies successfully. Knowing that undergraduates has more than a thousand students in each batch, the Senate agreed to a "one class, one representative" way so that, a representative could go on stage to receive the graduation certificate during convocation.

At that time, my academic result ranked seventh in the class, with an average of more than 80 points. The direct entry requirement for master's degree was an undergraduate whose academic result were the top 10 of their class and he or she should be from the same coursework program within the same faculty. Or else, a written entry assessment and interview would be carried out before the postgraduate program. In addition, if one of the top ten undergraduates has no interest to continue to pursue his or her master's degree by coursework or research program directly, the student who was ranked the eleventh position will automatically qualify for the direct entry to a master's degree without any written assessment or interview.

Knowing that I was feeling homesick I could not wait to fly back to my home town. I let go of the direct entry privilege of continuing masters degree. I decided to give it away to my classmate who was ranked eleventh. I rang my classmate who was ranked eleventh.

"Yu, I have something to tell you..."

"Chen, please go ahead. Is there anything I can help you with?" His tone full of care and concern.

"Well, you know I have the privilege to continue to master's degree as offered by our faculty, but I really miss my home. I plan to get a long term full time job in my home town, hoping I can contribute a bit to my family's finance. Since my younger brother is entering his second year in a private university, his tuition fee is three times more than ours. Furthermore, my grandmother is aging, I really miss her and long to spend time with her."

"In actual fact, Taiwan degree isn't recognized by Malaysia, so I have no plans to continue my master's degree in Taiwan."

"I am so grateful for the care and love of my classmates and friends for the past four to five years, all of you have made my dream come true of studying abroad."

I continued my conversation, "So, I'm calling you today to tell you that you can take my slot to enter directly for your master's degree, since you are at the eleventh place in our class. Please don't waste the ten slot offered by our faculty! Two years later, I promise to come and attend your master's degree convocation, ok?"

"Really? Wow! This is really a mixed feeling. I really thank you for giving me this chance of direct entry, thank you! Thank you! I will never forget this for all my life. On the other hand, we will miss each other for a while. You must come back to visit us after two years, ok! "Yu said.

"Sure. Roger that. *'Jia You'* and see you." I said it with an indescribable sadden heart.

After a long discussion, my class committee reached a decision about who would be the representative to go on stage and receive the graduation certificate during convocation. They assigned a spokesman to call me up.

"Chen Chen, our class has decided," said the spokesperson.

"What has been decided? Can I still offer my help to anyone before I go back to my hometown?" I responded politely.

"Well, our class unanimously decided, and appointed you as our representative to go on stage and receive the graduation certificate on our behalf." The spokesperson made a statement and sounded like a sergeant in the army.

"No, no, I am not qualified. I am neither the first in the class nor a student with outstanding performance. I am just the President of this year's undergraduate magazine only," I refused.

"Listen, please listen to me …Decision is final, and it is definitely our wish too. You know our class has 52 students and 48 have decided to pursue their master's degree in our faculty. In other words, they all have the opportunity to go on stage to receive their master's degrees certificate one by one…"

I interrupted him.

"But, after excluding me, there are still three more classmates, who did not take the master's degree, and they are local students. I have to go back anyway, it doesn't matter to me! I'm sorry ..." This time, it was him who did not wait for me to end my conversation but just interrupted me.

"That's why everyone nominated me to convey our final decision to you. Between you and me, and two other female classmates, you have the best grades among the four of us! Moreover, you are going back soon. That's why you should represent everyone which means a lot to yourself and us. Furthermore, the three of us fully agreed without any objection."

"By the way, the committee acknowledges your valid concern and doubt about such decision, you may think it might be a "back door" arrangement, that's why they nominate me to convey the good news to you. But, it's our class's honor to have you chosen, you really deserve it, you are the one!" He affirmed the message.

''Em...Indeed the best and most precious gift before I go back. My father is also coming over to attend my convocation. I believe he will be very proud of me.''

"Alright then. Thank you for the confirmation, and thank you for everyone's love and care for me. Two years later, I will definitely attend everyone's master's degree convocation." I smiled happily.

Right after this, I ran to the University 's Overseas Students Affairs Association to report on such a moment of honor and glory. Suddenly, I fell into silence again.

"Eh.. It is a good news to rejoice about, why do you look sad again?" Madam Lo puzzled.

"Yes, now I'm worried about the limited budget I have to buy a dignified dress. You know that I usually wear T-shirts and trouser, as it is easier for me to ride on a bike or bicycle to move around. A decent and proper long skirt cannot be found in my closet." I spoke softly.

"Oh! I originally wanted to give the beautiful long dress to you and PaoPao a day before the convocation after washing it. Since you mentioned it now, I won't be able to surprise you but to disclose it to you first. Don't worry about the dress, it's settled." Madam Lo comforted me.

"Really? Madam Lo is always the best! Thank you! How can I ever repay you ?" I asked cheerfully.

"Keeping in touch after your convocation is the best pay back," said Madam Lo.

"Okay, okay! Sure, sure! See you tomorrow!"

Finally came the big day of the convocation, it was held outdoors in the evening. Everything went on smoothly. When it was my class's turn, I wore an all-white flowing skirt and walked steadily on the stage. I received the bundle of certificates on behalf of my classmates from the Minister of Education in Taiwan. Facing the cameras, I posed for 3 seconds. After taking pictures, I was ready to step down from the stage.

The entire process took not more than thirty seconds, but it definitely marked a great milestone in my life. It was very important and had a significant positive impact on me. It will forever be a remarkable thirty seconds.

3 WEEKS

When I went abroad to study, it was a suitcase with 20kg luggage. When I returned home after my undergraduate convocation, it was still the same suitcase with 20kg luggage weight.

The only difference was that the luggage going abroad was full of authentic local food and daily necessities such as Milo, cereals, hangers and laundry detergent bars. When I returned home, it was full of textbooks.

I was grateful that I could afford to buy myself a return air ticket to celebrate Chinese New Year at my hometown during winter holiday over the last few years. Also, I managed to bring back most of the textbooks. However, only my purple winter coat and a white-washed blue quilt that accompanied me during my four to five years in Taiwan was sacrificed and abandoned during my last trip. I was in tears, sleepless for several nights just thinking about parting with my purple winter coat and light blue quilt. I would soon have to give them away by dropping them off at the Overseas Affairs Association Office on the day prior to my departure. I couldn't bear to give it away but I knew I had to pass it on to the new freshmen who would need it.

Finally, with only 100 Taiwan dollars (about RM10 only) left in my bank account, I quietly said goodbye with a saddened heart to Formosa Island.

Once I was back in Kuching, the first thing to do was to embrace the local delicious food. They were none other than Laksa and Kolo Mee.

Next, check out job vacancy via all possible sources such as newspapers and internet, and actively applying by sending out my resume.

Knowing that I could go home every day and enjoy the warmth of my home sweet home, I only intended to live in this small city named Kuching. With that, I could also spend time and accompany my elderly grandmother and parents whom I missed for several years. Furthermore, my elder sister had just married a Taiwanese that year, and my younger brother had furthered his study to Taiwan two years ago. If I still remained overseas, I could not imagine how much burden my parents would have without me. At least, I could help take my grandmother for regular doctor's appointment or sometimes give her a ride round the city.

That's the main reason why I did not apply for a job outside of Kuching.

Resuming my own way of meditation practice since I was a child, I prayed that I would find a permanent job and a dream company to work with as soon as possible. It's time to contribute and add value to the family.

Waiting for an unknown future reminded me of the tough moments while I was waiting for the application results to study abroad in Taiwan after secondary school graduation. The difference was, I could not engage any fortune-teller, nor could I complain or blame my destiny. On the contrary, I was full of confidence, waiting patiently, and applying for all potential job vacancies aggressively. I rehearsed in mind how I would respond during interviews, in order to win the employer's attention and gain an employment offer.

Ring. . Ring. . The phone rang. The number displayed on the screen was not found in my handphone's contact list. It was an unfamiliar fixed line phone number with a Kuching area code in front of it. Knowing this phone called during daytime, there should be no harm, so I just picked it up.

"Hello, is this Chen Chen?" The lady asked in fluent English.

"Hello, hi. Yes. I am." I answered in English too.

"I'm calling from the human resources department on behalf of a silicon company. Tomorrow at ten o'clock in the morning, can you attend a job interview at the lobby of the Riverside Hotel? Please look for Miss Rose. Your interview is scheduled at 10:15 in the morning. May I know if can you come for the interview?" She explained in English.

"Ok! OK! No problem, see you tomorrow, thank you." I was overjoyed.

The next morning, I departed at 9 o'clock and arrived at 9:30. The so-called early bird catches the worm. I believed if I arrived early, I could settle down my emotions and familiarize myself with the surroundings to make myself more confident.

I was interviewed by two high position individuals. One was the Vice President of Operations and the other was the Senior Manager of Operations. Nevertheless, during the interview, I carried myself with confidence and positive attitude. The questions and answers were straightforward, and I brought all my personal documents such as final project of all subjects, bachelor's degree certificate and university transcript.

"Each subject has a final year project in a group of four?" The senior manager asked.

"Yes, our final year project is not a one person one assignment only. Our faculty promotes team work, therefore every subject has a final year team project, at least 3 to 4 students in a team. The purpose of our professors was to train us to value teamwork and equip us prior to working life in the corporate world that requires inter-department effort to get the job done." I explained.

Although the two high position interviewers were experienced leaders in the related industry, they were kind and humble to me. The most important thing was they recognized my academic qualification and abilities, and they knew and understood my university's standard and achievement among higher education institution. Without them, I would not be offered a dream job with good remuneration just three weeks after I return from Taiwan.

"Her bachelor's degree is not accredited in Malaysia, and we can't recruit her ..." I overheard the dialogue between the head of human resources and the vice president, because the tone of their voices was a little agitated from the meeting room next to them.

"It's okay, we are not a government department, we are a private sector. As long as we recognize her ability, her attitude, and her academic qualification, we can give her a letter of employment! You may let her report to work directly next week ". I also heard the conversation from the vice president who fought for my right.

After fifteen minutes. . .

"Chen Chen, please come here to sign your letter of appointment. Please read the details carefully before signing. If you don't understand, please ask me. If you want to take it back or you need longer time to read through, please let me know so that I can change the date of report duty...." "The HR manager explained in detail.

"Okay. I'll read through it now. I'll ask you if I have any question. I can sign it right here. I don't need to bring it back. Thank you." I made up my mind on the spot, as if he would change his mind and I would miss the job opportunity if I brought it back home.

After five minutes. . .

"Mr. Mali, I read through and fully understand. I've signed on both copies too. Is it one copy for you and one copy for me?" I asked boldly without any fear.

"Yes, that's right. Please report to our office on Monday, August 3rd at 8:30 in the morning. The address is as specified in the letter of employment. The probation period is three months. Five working days with two days off. Your job title, remuneration and benefits are as stated in the letter of employment too. Please remember to bring your IC as you need to open a new bank account for our company to facilitate payroll every month end and etc..". The human resources manager explained further in details as part of the standard procedure for a new hire.

"OK! OK! I fully understand. I will definitely report at 8.30am on August 3rd."

My prayer was answered. I got my first full-time job in just three weeks. It's awesome! I would never forget him, who affirmed and recruited me within 30 minutes of interview only. Without him who fought for me, my career path might be completely different. The company was a new start up who was doing a mass recruitment to form an organized team.

Since then, I have served in that company and other companies in the similar industry for nearly two decades. And throughout all these year, I have not seen the company recruit fresh graduates from Taiwan. Even overseas students from Taiwan with relevant work experiences were rare and only a handful of them were hired too.

ONE YEAR ONE NEW COUNTRY

Ever since working full time in Kuching, I reflected and set for myself a personal recreation goal of "One Year One New Country". Literally, it meant I would visit a new country every year. Revisiting the same place or country was not counted, the goal was one year one new country.

In 1999, I was one of the lucky ones chosen to be part of the forty persons in the start-up core elite team to join a technology transfer training that was held in Japan. From Monday to Friday, I paid attention in training center, but when it came to the weekend, some of my teammates and I, took the bullet train and visited Tokyo Disneyland, Ginza, Nagoya, Osaka and any recreation tourist spot that we could plan ahead. I was so grateful that our accommodation was fully sponsored by the company. We were also paid travel allowance too. That's the reason why I could spend on sightseeing and food hunting every weekend.

In 2000, after coming back from technology training in Japan, my life was so tied up to work. I was part of a big team that was working on establishing new procedures and putting many things into place for a new factory to be handed over to us once construction was complete. Therefore, I could barely plan to travel anywhere but just made a trip to Taiwan something I had promised my classmates in university two years ago. I promised

I would attend their master's degree convocation and take group pictures with them. Hmm! I gave in and classified Taiwan as one of my "new" country under my "One Year One New Country" travel goals that I set after working full time in Kuching.

In 2001, I visited New Zealand. The main reason why I chose New Zealand was because I never met my BFF (best friend forever) after she left us in Middle School time to pursue her studies in New Zealand. She then settled down there by getting a job and set up her family there. On her wedding day, I could not afford the travel expenses, but also encountered the busiest peak season of my work. Therefore, I made plans to visit her at the end of the year when there were many holidays such as Christmas and New Year, and the work schedule was slower during that period too. At the same time, I planned to visit my uncle and his family who had settled down in New Zealand after studying abroad since 1970's.

2002 marks a significant and really important milestone in my life. I started dating a guy who would become my life partner. We had our first date in May and we proceeded to register our marriage on Christmas Eve at the end of the year. Our close friends and relatives thought something "happened" on us. Why get married in such a hurry? So rush? Or whatever? No, not at all! Indeed, it was love at first sight for us. Furthermore, we were matured and old enough to form our own family. I actually hoped to get married before my 30's. Looking at myself who was exceeding the marriageable age, soon I would be classified as high-risk pregnant woman in a few years. Actually, to tie the knot it takes two families to say "Yes" and my sweetheart's family was giving us pressure to get married as if I would become a "runaway bride" if marriage was procrastinated.

My 2002 "One Year One New Country" travel plan was to visit Singapore. To be precise, it was a 4 days 3 nights "buy one free one" cruise package where Singapore was the boarding and berthing port. My sweetheart and I decided on this value for money package as we were mainly attracted by the "eat all you can", six meals a day, which perfectly matched our situation of limited budget while preparing for a wedding ahead of us. You see my sweetheart at that time was tall and skinny, it would definitely be a great opportunity for him to put on some weight to look good for our wedding photo shooting.

Ha!Ha! Indeed he put on weight, as much as six kilograms. However, the major setback of this value for money, economy package was the cruise cabin was enclosed without any window. I usually have car sick or sea sick, which made me feel into dizzy and discomfort if I stayed inside the cabin. Therefore, we just hung out and had fun, rushing from one entertainment event to another. At the end of the day, we dragged our over exhausted body to bed and just fell asleep till the next day.

In January of the year 2003, we had our wedding reception, a wedding feast for friends and relatives, officiated the tea ceremony, and officially moved into his house with a new title, "Wife". But before that, my 2003 "One Year One New Country" travel plan was deliberately brought forward to December 2002, to the Sultanate of Oman in the Middle East, with a transition in Dubai. Though it was only a business trip, I considered that my recreation plan fulfilled as it's truly a new country to visit.

In 2004, I had yet to plan any travelling trip as I was pregnant. I had severe morning sickness during the first two months. Life was miserable as I almost took half day leave every day during my first trimester of pregnancy. Knowing this was my first child, I took extra caution by not making any travels through air flight or cruise and etc. I just lived a routine and normal life until I gave birth to my firstborn.

On January of 2005, my labour astonished the nurses and doctors in the delivery room because my baby was naturally delivered;

fast and exciting. The reason was because my waters had broke (known as amniotic fluid). When we rushed to reach the hospital, it was only six o'clock in the morning. The nurse upon checking me had seen the baby's head exposed. I clearly remember what the nurse said:

"Hold on! Don't inhale and exhale hard. The doctor hasn't arrived yet. We can't proceed."

"You can see the baby's head, why can't I deliver the baby? Hurry up and call the doctor la!!" The contraction pain drove me crazy.

"Mam, please do not push. Because your pregnancy is only 35.5 weeks and full term is 36 weeks, according to our hospital labour ward rules & regulations, none full term labour can only proceed with the presence of the pediatrician and gynecologist, otherwise the hospital will not be responsible for any consequences." The nurse said.

Thanks to two diligent doctors, they were present within 20 minutes.

I inhaled and exhaled, and push hard. Doctors followed up by a cut, and my baby was born; smooth and quick. The gynecologist cut the umbilical cord, patted the baby, and we heard "wah wah" the loud cries from my newborn baby daughter.

"Mum is in good health." My gynecologists said after the placenta was discharged and done with the stitching.

"Baby is normal too." The pediatrician said, and place my baby daughter in my hands gently.

My darling husband witnessed the entire labor process. He has phobia of seeing fresh blood since his childhood, his face turned pale and his hands were freezing cold. Thankfully he heard our baby's cries before he fainted due to an overwhelming first live experience as new parents in the labour room. Indeed, it was an unforgettable joy for us as new parents.

After a full month in confinement, while I still on maternity leave for another whole month, my hubby and I visited Bali Island in Indonesia to fulfill my "One Year One New Country" travel plan. It served as our reward and an encouragement to us who were just newly promoted to parents.

In 2006, when my daughter was one year old, we decided to visit a nearby oil rich country - Brunei Darussalam. Apart from fulfilling my "One Year One New Country" travel plan, it was also our first trip to visit my Aunt (my mother's sister) and her family ever since she married to a man in Brunei many years ago. We could not wait to share our newborn joy with her. We were grateful that my aunt was still in good health and as extrovert as before. She always humble herself before God. She often evangelized to me through her own testimony. She tried to share about God to me.

In 2007, it was another turning point in my life. That year, I did not want to visit any new country, I just wanted to conquer the highest peak of South East Asia, the four thousand-meter-high, Low's peak on Mount Kinabalu in Sabah, Borneo Island. Thanks to my hubby who not only accompanied me, he also carried the backpack up and down the Mountain. With that, we saved sixty Malaysia Ringgit for pick-up service. My hubby was also my personal body guard as the entire team were participated by all the males. Great to have such lifetime companion.

In 2008, I missed my Hong Kong roommate so much We became close while we were studying together for the Preparatory Program at National Normal University, Linkou campus in Taiwan back in year 1993. At that time, she was a devoted Christian who often evangelized to me. After graduating for so many years,

I realized I missed her so much. Especially during this season for me who just encountered God and born again spiritually. I wanted to share my salvation and good news with her face to face. Furthermore, she has been married for many years and I had yet to congratulate her and her spouse in person. I felt I must make a trip to visit her that year, I also would like to introduce my hubby to her too.

During this trip, my husband and I touched down at Macau, took the boat to Hong Kong, and then travelled to Guangzhou by train. Later we finally returned to Macau for departure back to Kuching. The best foods during our trip was the Hong Kong dim sum and Macau Portuguese egg tarts. I missed that so much that I wish we would visit the same place again.

In 2009, when my daughter was five years old, we were so blessed by the launching of the new Kuala Lumpur - Sydney route offered by Air Asia Low Cost Airlines. I stayed in front of my computer an hour before midnight, aiming and prayed to grab three zero-price tickets. Wow! Thank God for His provision! I managed to grab three zero-price tickets to serve as my husband and I's belated fifth anniversary wedding celebration! Of course, we also used the opportunity to visit several good friends of mine from Middle School. They furthered their study in Australia and settled down there as permanent residents. In addition, I also prayed that I would get pregnant again after this relaxing trip.

Indeed God answered my prayer, I was pregnant after returning from Australia.

In 2010, after celebrating my second child's full month baby shower, I started to work in a new foreign investment company. Again, I was the pioneer batch for the start-up company. One of my main tasks was being responsible for arranging 80 employees, including myself to be trained and accommodated in the United

States. Again, we paid attention from Monday to Friday during the training, and the weekend was our fun and happy time again. This time, I committed myself to attend Sunday Service at the church nearby on Sunday morning. I also met a lot of brothers and sisters in Christ there. So, we went to lunch together and toured around St. Louis Arch and Jefferson National Park. I felt the warmth of these brothers and sisters. Indeed, God's love has no boundary, even though we had only met for the first time in a foreign country.

In 2011, the company that I worked with was busy with intensive import and export on top of the endless recruitment and employee training due to company expansion. Amazingly, I was pregnant with my third child during the busy peak season. Considering my age, I was categorized as a high-risk pregnant woman. My morning sickness was overwhelming, much tougher than the previous two children. But by God's grace and mercy, I had inner peace and joy over my temporary physical discomfort.

In 2012, after giving birth to our third child, we planned a trip to Cambodia towards the end of my maternity leave in order to make up for the fulfillment of Year 2011 "One Year One New Country" travel plan. This time, the Angkor Wat and French Toast were the most memorable experience.

At the end of 2012, we visited South Korea to mark our tenth anniversary of our marriage. Nami Island, the famous site of the famous Korean drama, "Winter Sonata". It was definitely on my places to visit list after longing to visit for decades. We were amazed by the advancements and convenient transportation in South Korea, the cleanliness and the beauty of the city. A ceramic bowl of ginseng chicken soup in the winter was fascinating and the tasty ginseng soup was imprinted in our memory forever.

During that year, I felt convicted about my personal recreation plan. I decided to surrender my "One Year One New Country" recreation plan into God's hand, I prayed and Holy Spirit touched my heart.

"It's time to turn personal plan into a family plan."

"I have bigger and better plan to bless you and your family."

"As long as it is a happy family trip blessed by God, there will be joy. Does not matter new country or new attraction."

Therefore, since 2013, I obeyed what God had convicted my heart. I no longer insisted on the personal recreation plan of traveling to a new country each year.

In 2013, my husband and I returned to Taiwan again to attend the fifteenth anniversary party of my graduation from university. In actual fact, it was a first visit for my hubby to Taiwan. It felt more fulfilling that the "One Year One New Country" plan this time was for my beloved one who was more joyful than for myself. During this time we also visited my ex-boss in Tainan.

In 2014, we revisited Brunei Darussalam with our two daughters. Indeed we were full of joy despite having two kids with us. We cherished the grandaunt and grandnieces moment so much. In addition, we dropped by Miri for few days to give our kids some "cousins bonding time" with our relatives. What a shame to realize that it was our first family trip to Miri. A place that is near yet so far to reach. However, a belated trip is better than never making it.

In 2015, we thank God for His provision, I managed to grab low-fare return tickets for my family of five to revisit Taiwan but it was the first visit for the kids to have lots of bonding time with their cousins, my sister's children. For me, I craved for my favorite food none other than deep fried crispy chicken chop and famous pearl milk tea. Shopping in various night markets was also full of joy as a family. It was totally not an issue even though I was revisiting the same country again.

In 2016, I thank God for His provision again, I managed to grab two low-fare air ticket to Vietnam for five days four nights short trip with my hubby. In the middle of our trip, we took a 33 hours long journey train from Hanoi to Ho Chi Minh City. We visited Halong Bay, a must-visit World Heritage Site. We also visited the Vietnam War Museum, we felt empathy and sad in our hearts by the things we saw.

However, the most impressive experience was the thunder storm and flash floods in the urban area, which caused our bus to detour and arrive very late at the hotel. Not forgetting the non-stop vehicles honking on the road. We witnessed the cultural differences of more than 90% women diligently working in the market place, as well as the potential that Vietnam has among the ASEAN countries; the potentials, capabilities and efforts to catch up in terms of economy and development as a country.

In 2017, we thank God again for the supply through Air Asia Airlines. We managed to travel to Maldives using low-fare air tickets. We reached Male, the capital of Maldives very late at night. My youngest sister-in-law helped us to book a water villa at a five-star hotel with mega discounted member price too. Imagined you just walked to the water villa's balcony and jumped into the crystal clear warm seawater, surrounded by a group of small fish, it was really worth the trip. We went cycling around the island, enjoyed the sea breeze, walked on the snowy white sand, gazed at the sunrise and sunset, enjoyed barbecue seafood by the beach and many more. Our hearts were filled with thankfulness and gratitude, a bonus to nourish our husband-wife relationship in our fifteenth wedding anniversary.

In 2018, one of our very close sister in Christ was encouraged by us to study in Taiwan. We promised to visit her during her studies. Seeing that she was graduating in 2018, our family, five of us kept our promise to congratulate her in Kaohsiung just before her convocation. Again, we were blessed with low-fare air tickets and set off on our four day three night short family trip. We spent whole day in I-Shou Theme Park. It was really worth the visit and value for money, because the theme park was not occupied with many visitors and our kids were queuing for the same rides or facilities again and again. Their laughter and screaming brought me back to my innocent but memorable childhood. Amazing and sweet.

In 2019, our family of five managed to grab zero-fare air tickets. We brought the kids to Legoland Theme Park in Johor Bahru. We soaked ourselves in the water park until the park closed for the day. We got so tan, our skin turned to become like roasted duck. Again, seeing my kids repeatedly jumping up and down on the hot staircase heated up by the hot sun with their bare foot, queuing for the same facilities and sliding down, was a joy. I thank God for His blessing and protection.

GRANDMA'S ROOMMATE

Before I got married, although I worked hard and saved money to fulfill my "one year one new country" travel plans, my daily life was normal and ordinary. I kept it as close to home as possible just so that I can stay close to my grandma who was old and ill. Because I had missed once when I found my grandpa experiencing a stroke in bed with his mouth full of white foam and couldn't get up early in the morning, I told myself I would not let it happen again on my grandma. She who waited patiently until I came back home after almost five years studying abroad. The only way I thought I could pay back was to be my grandma's roommate. Yes, that is to sleep with her every night.

Another valid reason was my parent's master bedroom was upstairs, only grandma was staying in the room downstairs alone at night due to her limited physical movement and for easy access. Apart from my parents and grandma, nobody stayed at home except me. My dad's siblings all married and moved out, and so did my elder sister. My younger brother was studying abroad at that time too.

Apart from the ordinary office working life from Monday to Friday, Saturday and Sunday were the happiest time for my grandma and I. I was her driver and she would just give me the schedule and itinerary. We often go to the clinic or hospital for regular appointment. The next popular hot spots were wet market, grocery shops nearby, houses of grandma's relatives and etc.

At that time, a 600CC Kancil, Malaysian-made car was passed on to me by my sister after she got married in Taiwan. However, Kuching as a city in Borneo Island is full of tropical rainforest, experienced 2,500 mm rainfall yearly. Kuching not only rained almost every day, flash floods easily covered the main roads due to under developed infrastructure nearby our area.

In view of my short height, I prayed to have a jeep or 4WD, which was slightly higher and has a wider space. Thinking it could be more convenient for bringing grandma during weekend, after returning from training in Japan, I bought my first Jeep. It was a second-hand fully reconditioned blue jeep imported from Japan.

At the beginning, grandma still had the strength to raise herself by her own feet and step into the jeep.

At the later stage, my grandma became weaker. When she had to go to the hospital every month for blood transfusion, I could only use my dad's Proton Saga salon car to send her.

Both Grandma and Grandpa's character were totally opposite from each other as if they were from different planet. Grandpa was extroverted, outspoken and short-tempered whereas Grandma was introverted and gentle. Grandpa was expressive and very emotionally oriented whereas Grandma was calm and reserved.

Therefore, even when Grandma was very sick, she endured the pain without showing out any negative feeling. Sometimes, I realized that my "silence is gold" character was most likely inherited from my grandma especially when I was facing tough and difficult times in life.

I still remember that there was once a blood transfusion, my grandma suddenly had an abnormal convulsion. Later, it was confirmed that the hospital negligently transfused wrong type yet incompatible blood type.

Though Grandma's life was preserved and alive, her health was deteriorating.

FOREVER PAIN

"Grandma, this Christmas and New Year's Eve, I'm going to New Zealand. I will visit uncle Steve and his family for the first time in New Zealand. I will visit my BFF(best friend forever) who just married to New Zealand too." I told my grandma in Teochew dialect.

"Very good! Little Chen. I will give you a big angpao (known as red pocket in Chinese tradition) to enjoy your trip!" Grandma's love is one that no words can describe.

"Ah Mah, you have to take care of yourself and wait for me to come back. For the upcoming Chinese New Year, I will give you a big angpao too. I can't take so much money from you la!"

For my 2001-2002 "One Year One New Country" travel plan, a New Year Count down trip was carried out as scheduled. First I went to North Island, stayed at my uncle's house for a few days, then joined the local tour group with my best friend and set off to South Island.

When reaching the resort town, Queenstown at South Island, I suddenly received a phone call from my uncle.

"Chen, I'm going back to Kuching first. Your grandma most likely can't make it!" Came the shocking news from afar.

"WHAT!" I couldn't help myself, burst into tears and couldn't speak for a long time.

"What should I do? I ... I'll ask ... I can ask the tour guide ... Can ...find the way for me ... to go back with you?" My vision was blurred, tears filled and blocked by my eyes, my vocal chords stuck, my emotional and logical thinking all chaotic and confused.

"Mr. Tour Guide, I beg you, can you help me, find a way to go back to Auckland, North Island now?" I cried and begged the tour guide.

Our tour package was a budgeted trip, meaning the tour guide was the driver too since he could speak Mandarin. He drove us in a minivan, a total 12 of us including himself. He was indeed very exhausted after driving the van for a long day. Furthermore, it was late in the evening, the travel agency was not only closed, almost every shop and operation was closed to celebrate Christmas and the New Year. The tour guide was unable to reach out to his travel agency in North Island, and he was not familiar with how to get an air ticket to fly me from the South Island to North Island alone. In fact, I didn't dare to hop on any public transport in the middle of the night. I was unfamiliar but actually bold enough to take a risk, as this was already the second last day of the trip.

But, in order not to affect the good mood of other fellow travelers, I could only follow the team in silence. I silently hoped and prayed in my own way that my grandma could hold on till I came back. I still owed her a big angpao. How could she leave without saying goodbye to her "room mate"?

My uncle could not wait for me, so he rushed to the airport alone, queuing up on the waiting list. He was on "stand-by" mode from one flight to another flight, finally someone was absent and it was his turn on the waiting list to get the seat. Uncle managed to meet grandma and say good bye to her.

On my way back from South Island to Auckland, Uncle called again.

"Little Chen, grandma passed away. The funeral is scheduled on January 2. You have time to pay your last respect." It was my mom who used my uncle's phone to call me.

"Wah! I will touch down in the late evening of January 1 and the funeral is on the 2nd?" I burst into tears and my emotions went out of control because of the sadness in my heart.

I never expect, the conversation prior my New Zealand trip was actually a farewell to grandma. I believed Grandma knew her end time was near, she didn't say it out simply because she used to keep the hurt and suffering, pain and bitterness to herself. She even blessed me with a big angpao.

My grandma, my roommate. It was sad to face the fact that eventually I still missed the opportunity to accompany her till her last breath.

My New Zealand trip, forever pain.

PRELUDE TO THE INVISIBLE LOVE

When I was 33 years old, the mid-2007 to early 2008, was a turning point in my life.

Ever since returning from Taiwan in 1998, I only invested my time in working so hard at the market place on top of making my "One Year One New Country" recreation plan into reality. This was followed by the norm of settling down; getting married to my Mr. Right, bearing children, to owning our first home sweet home and own vehicles to move around.

Frankly speaking, such a smooth sailing and fruitful life style seemed to be a dream life for fresh graduates and young couples to pursue. A lifestyle and living standard that a small family and newly promoted parents longed for. An above average living with nothing to complain about.

However, when I found no lack in material things, I realized there was an emptiness in my soul, something lacking that I could not explain in words but could feel it within me. I recalled the moment when I used to meditate, pray, wish or hope for everything I desired for. True enough, after my meditation in my mind, a warm force often swept through and within me to push me to keep moving ahead, to never give up. Each times those prayers or desires were answered, I responded with a grateful and loving heart.

When I was thirty-three years old, this invisible force became stronger and stronger, and it seemed that I would be brought before Him.

"Chen, I just attended the first lesson of "Parenting with Confidence". It was great. Will you go with me to the next class?" My BFF who came back from New Zealand, brought her daughter back for kindergarten final year in Kuching and signed up for this newly conducted course in the kindergarten.

"Great! I am also looking for similar courses, because my daughter is going to kindergarten next year. We must master parenting skills, be well prepared ahead of our children, guide them, and lead them towards the right path." I was as excited as if exploring a new discovery on earth.

Without hesitation, I attended the second lesson with my BFF. At the end of the course, we celebrated the course completion/ graduation and had fellowship at the lecturer's house.

During the class, I occasionally heard the course coordinator called the lecturer "pastor". At that time, I really didn't know what "pastor" mean. I was not interested in asking questions or exploring further either.

However, this wonderful and invisible love came to my mind again at the lecturer's home during the fellowship. I asked:

"Every time I encounter difficulties or desire for something, I will meditate. Then, an invisible and wonderful power comforted my heart and motivated me to move on. Why is this happening?"

"This is your prayer to Heavenly Father. He created you, He knows you and He loves you even when you are in your mother's womb. This invisible love is God's amazing and unconditional love." The lecturer explained.

At the same time, the lecturer asked his wife to take out a booklet in the room and handed it to me.

"This booklet, please bring it back with you, read it with an open heart. If that invisible love touches you again after reading the last paragraph, shall we meet again and further understand this amazing and invisible love of God?" The lecturer explained clearly.

"Okay! Okay! I'll make appointment with you after reading it. Thank you." I promised.

That night, I read it again and again, but I did not understand very well. At the end of the last paragraph, I read several times wholeheartedly, and I did not understand very well too. But this invisible love took away my anxiety instantly, filled my inner emptiness instantly with indescribable peace and joy.

If you have chosen to believe and receive the eternal life God offers then here is ...

A Sample Prayer

"Dear Lord Jesus,

I thank you for the GOOD NEWS that has been made clear to me. I acknowledge that I am a sinner in need of your help.

I believe in you, that you died on the cross and rose from the dead to pay the penalty for my sins. I accept you as my personal Lord and Saviour. I receive the eternal life you promise me as a believer.

I now choose to worship you alone as my God. Please help me from this point on to fully trust you in every way in my life.

In your Holy Name I pray. Amen."

"Lecturer, I have finished reading the booklet you gave me. Especially the last paragraph, I read and read again. What should I do next? What materials should I read?" When I met the lecturer again, I couldn't wait to ask about the peace and joy brought by this invisible love.

"Congratulations on your choice to accept Jesus as your Lord and Savior. This amazing and invisible love is also the Grace of God. Because of His Agape love, God gave His only son Jesus, who came to the world and was crucified on the cross for our sin. Jesus redeemed our sin and by His blood we are set free. Jesus resurrected on the third day, symbolize our belief in Him and we will be born again spiritually."

"Next, I encourage you to continue to get to know this amazing and loving God. I will arrange a sister in Christ to guide you on the 'Essentials of New Life', it's a guideline for new Christians like you, okay?" said the lecturer.

"Okay! Okay! By the way, lecturer, why does Ms. Jane call you pastor? Excuse me, what does pastor mean?" I asked ignorantly, a question on my mind for more than half a year.

"I serve full-time in the church, like a shepherd leading a flock of sheep. I also disciple my sheep to read Bible, understand God's Word, and build relationship with Him. So, a shepherd plus a disciple, you can call me pastor. You are one of my lost sheep that Jesus is looking for a long time. Thank God. Praise the Lord. You accepted salvation." Pastor responded patiently.

"Yeah ... Pastor, thank you, Pastor ... I ... I will work hard to know my Savior ..." I am grateful, but there were thousands of questions in my new born mind. Why shepherd? Why sheep? What is salvation? What is redemption? Salvation, born again, disciple. . .

"Chen Chen, congratulations once again, we continue to grow in God's word. Indeed God's love is invisible, but you can feel His unconditional love with your heart; have faith and hope. Before we end, shall my spouse and I pray for you?" Pastor asked.

"Okay! Okay!" I look forward to this new life experience.

"Dear Heavenly Father, thank You for bringing Chen Chen to our 'Parenting with Confidence' course, thank You for Your grace, she is saved and has accepted You as her Savior. Lord! Thank you so much for Chen Chen's desire and search for you, the invisible love in her since she was in kindergarten. Lord! We commit Chen Chen into Your hands, we pray that You lead her, guide her, protect her and her family. Lord! We also pray that Your wisdom be upon her, as she will be disciple by our sister in Christ of our church. Pray that she will complete 'The Essential New Life' and establish a relationship with You at all times. We pray that she reads the Bible. O Lord! Once again, we give thanks for Chen Chen's salvation, Heaven is full of joy with her salvation, we give all this glory to You, our God. We pray in Jesus Almighty name, Amen." Indeed a long prayer from pastor.

"Thank you!" At that time, I didn't know that I should respond with "Amen".

It was the end of year 2007, I accepted Jesus Christ as my Savior, this invisible love deep in my heart since I was very young, He is someone truly has amazing and unconditional love. Ever since then, every day I live by faith and hope. No fear but trust in Him when I am in trial and difficulties. Glory to God for whatever success or blessings from Him.

After believing in Jesus Christ, God spoke to me through a character in the Bible, the prophet Jeremiah, in the book of Jeremiah chapter 1 verse 5:

> "Before I made you in your mother's womb, I chose you. Before you were born, I set you apart for a special work. I appointed you as a prophet to the nations."

Yes, God has plans for prophet Jeremiah. Likewise, God has plans for you and I, each and everyone.

I recall the moment, when although I have never really known Jesus, nor accepted Him as my Lord Savior, and did not know how to trust in Him for all things, He has been guiding me to the specific place He has designated in my life journey. In order to find my destiny, I must be able to work diligently to carry out God's will and plan for me. It depends on my ability and determination to obey and follow Him completely.

In my growing life journey, I often pray and meditate on something I desire for, which was actually His grace, the ability to desire God's promise and plan for me, together with my diligent hard work, God answered my prayer.

Later, God's spoke to me again through His words in Psalm 139, verses 13 to 16, affirming that my ability to meditate on desirable things from an early age was actually the destiny God had prepared for me even I was in my mother's womb.

> 13 You made my whole being.
>   You formed me in my mother's body.
> 14 I praise you because you made me in an amazing and
>   wonderful way.
>   What you have done is wonderful.
>   I know this very well.
> 15 You saw my bones being formed
>   as I took shape in my mother's body.
>   When I was put together there,
> 16 you saw my body as it was formed.
>   All the days planned for me
>   were written in your book
>   before I was one day old.

My new life after believing in Him, O Lord, has too many testimonies to share. . . (to be continued)

隐形的爱
INVISIBLE LOVE
诞生-成长 BORN & GROWN UP

真真 Chen Chen

目录

诞生了

话说 1974 年的某个良辰吉日，我在婆罗洲的一个小镇的政府医院诞生了。

犹记得妈妈常回忆到，她床位隔壁待产的孕妇趕在我出世前先被推进产房生了。当她与新生儿被推出来时，把我妈给吓得一度魂飛魄散，因为这男婴胎记是烙印在全身，除了臀部连脸部也如"包青天"般的绿。

紧接着，就是轮到我妈妈入產房準備催生了；终于，我平安顺利的诞生了，身上也有胎记。但是，非常感恩的是我只有臀部是"青春"的绿胎记，跟之前那一位比我早几分钟出世的男婴刚好相反。这胎记陪伴了我整整十一，二年，渐大惭淡，最终消失无踪，还我白里透红的臀肉。

家里给我取个乳名叫"小妹"，老人家相信有胎记的小孩健康又聪明。真的吗？有科学依据吗？事实是：听爷爷奶奶，爸爸妈妈说我从小好生好养，极少生病，天生左撇子，十个月大就会走路，眼睛会说话，伶牙俐齿，是逼迫也好，激励也可以，反正让爸爸成功戒烟的大功臣就是我，小真小妹，小妹小真。

就这样，我很快就五岁大，可以就读两年制幼稚园了。但我们不只是小康之家，还是三代同堂的大家庭，上有爷爷奶奶，加上我们三姐弟，爸妈为了节省开支，即便一个月学费只有马币 30,也是个经济负担，况且我又乖巧伶俐，所以就让我六岁才读一年制幼稚园。

人生的第一次

六岁那年，我开心上学去了。由于心智成熟，心态正确，学习成绩一直很优秀。又因为外表可爱出众，身高适中，被老师一眼选中成为幼稚园年度舞蹈表演队队员之一。

犹记得遴选过程中，老师在我们这群初选者当中示范几个舞步，让每个小朋友逐一演示，从中选出最适合的 12 位舞者。这将是我人生第一支舞，也会是我第一次登上舞台，怎么可以轻易放弃？至今，我还清楚记得，我不只很专注观察老师的舞步，轮到我演示时，更拼尽全力、脸带笑容，全神投入，跳出完美的舞步。

"小真，跳得真好！"

"等等，你现在是后排最后一位，看不到你啦。来！来！来到前排。。对。。往前一格。。。嗯。。我看看。。再上前一格。。。嗯。。再上一格。。。对。。。就是前排第二格位置。。"
舞蹈老师看见我的努力。

果然皇天不负有心人，我不只中选，老师还让我
排前排第二位，于是，"泥娃娃"—我人生第一支
舞就这样成了。

那一年幼稚园的家庭日，校方在两公里步行距离
的小学场地举办小朋友障碍赛。我参加的项目是
串珠比赛，我非常记得，本性认真，天真的我就
会专注，默想必胜。

"串完了，赶快跑到终点。。。加油！加油！"

"终点？什么是终点？哪里是终点？"我天真无
邪，不仅没见过真正的赛场，况且这么大的草
场，周围又站满人，大家又喊着给我加油，我真
的慌了！

我左顾右盼，总算看到妈妈在右边，就不管三七
二十一，锁定"妈妈"这一目标，就横向往右直
冲。

"小朋友，不是旁边，是前方！！请继续前进，冲向有一条红色丝带那里。"耳边传来老师的声音。

"為什麼要冲向那条红色丝带？"

我是百思不解，因为我一直以为红色丝带代表不可以超越；但是分秒必争，听到啥照办就是了。

"快点！快点！冲呀！冲向那条红色丝带！！"全场喊道。

就这样，在串珠比赛里，我不只串得最快，一粒不漏，还在数秒内，奋力冲向那条红色丝带，成功跑到终点。

就这样，我在串珠比赛里得到第一名。

哇！又是人生第一座奖杯；我心存感恩，当时攀上第一名领奖台阶的荣耀，至今还歷歷在目，也为我的幼小心灵种下丰硕的信心和美好回忆，无形中奠定了我一路走来，坚持专注，积极向上的品格。

卫生股长

隔年，我终于梦想成真，进入幼稚园当时障碍赛场地的小学就读一年级，终于可以天天到这么大的草场踏青晒太阳。回想起来，难怪长大后的我，脸上佈满雀斑，想必是小时候常暴露在阳光下的成果。

我被分配到一年级黄班，一如既往的认真态度，再加上会说话的双眸，很快又得到级任老师的青睐，不是选我当正副班长，而是卫生股长。原因是班上好几周的班级整洁比赛都"包尾"了，实在不光彩。这种要迎头赶上，一心求突破的坚持，务必要找一个积极进取的实践者。

"小真，老师选你当卫生股长。老师对你有信心，你一定可以胜任"。班导师走到我座位说道。

"好的！好的！我一定会让一黄班得班级整洁冠军"。我充满自信的说。

果然不负所望，到了周一的周会，当校长在台上报告一年级班级整洁比赛冠军是一黄班时，全班起立鼓掌，我更大步伐稳健走到台前，那时候多希望能有记者群不停对我"卡嚓"，拍照留念。

回到班上，大家谢谢我的领导，尤其老师那一番话至今仍清楚萦绕在耳边。

他说："老师没看错人，选你当卫生股长，就是知道你会把班上整洁搞好，谢谢你，继续加油!"

当时，我为每天的打扫工作重新选出一位可信赖负责人，再配几个平时與他/她比較配合的同學，而我自己負責星期二的打扫，就這樣，把全班分成五组，从周一到周五负责执行班上的整洁工作。

下课后，椅子全搬起来，打扫干净之后，把椅子归位。接着，用绳子把桌椅从左到右，从前到后拉直对齐。除了星期二我值勤之外，其他时候我也从旁协助，主要还是品质监督，确保每一天都是干净整齐的，这样，任何时间老师来打分都是满分的。

这里，我要感谢每天载送我们的鄰居阿姨，因为她的小车一次载送不完大家，所以要分两趟。我感谢她信任我，允许我乘搭第二趟的要求。考量小朋友的安全，通常小班要先载送，避免在校奔跑滋事。就这样，我成为班上每天最迟回家的那位，也确保我能有效执行卫生股长的任务。

我每天默想自己上台领奖的画面，终于心想事成，感恩所有信任我，配合我的老師，同學和鄰居阿姨。

陪我温习

我似乎与生俱来就是个积极认真的孩子。但凡承诺之事，都要做到最好。升上小学二年级，每天的晚自习，都哭哭啼啼，要求爸爸陪我温习的情景依然歷歷在目。

小時候的那個年代，补习是比較花錢的，家里沒有多餘的经费给我們補習。而我就读华小，除了课堂自购的书本，也沒有什么课外参考书或活动本，作业都是手写、抄黑板的。

我们家三代同堂，妈妈为了贴补家用，一天辛苦站上十二个小时，在当时唯一的购物广场当鞋店销售员，回到家也晚上十点了，更不用说陪小孩读書。

身为一家之主的爸爸也只是个普通公务员，眼看家里入不敷出，爸爸还兼差当个人寿保险代理，每晚都得晚上外出约见客户。爷爷奶奶又不识字，姐姐也只比我年长几岁，自己功课都应接不暇，那有时间教我，或说也懒得理我。

每晚爸爸要出去之际，我都泣不成声，央求他留下来教我做作业，帮忙温习功课，或者应付接下来的考试等等。尽管如此，為了生計爸爸还是狠下心出门赴约去了，只留下我坐在中厅椅子上。

这时的小小心灵又自我默想，化悲愤為力量，下定决心一定要考好成绩，才不糟蹋长辈的血汗钱，也不辜负他们的期望。

因此，我不再哭泣，也再沒有求助。于是，我上课认真听讲，不懂时大胆举手发问，由于一班有五十五个小朋友，有时候老师趕课不方便回答或详细解释，我便会趁休息时间去办公室问老师或同学，功课尽量在学校趕完。这种不耻下问，奋斗到底的精神终于见效了，我成绩突飞猛进，终于得了全班第九名。

果真，我默想得到个位数的心念又成了，感恩。

全场哗然

来到小学四年级的我，因为小学新开了一个体育项目的课外活动-排球，只限四年级或以上参加，且就读六年级的姐姐报名了，所以我也跟着报名。

基本上，报名的原因只有一个，就是那一天的下午就有得玩了，不必只呆在家里，挺无聊的。除了读书，就是温习功课。电视节目有限，卡通片播放也只有特定的时间。

可是问题来了。邻居阿姨第二轮载我们回到家都快两点了，如何趕在两点半又回到学校？

"小妹，下午一时半下课时，我们要请阿姨第一轮就先载我们回家。然后，你和我只有十五分钟冲凉，吃午饭和换运动装。因为，我们还要步行到香蕉路西段交差路口，一定要在两点十五分到达我朋友家，这样我们就可麻烦她妈妈一同载我们回学校。这样，两点半才能到学校，知道吗？"

姐姐继续说到：″要跟我，就要快点，知道吗？
不要拖啊！懂吗？″

″好的!好的!一定!一定!″我非常高兴，一口就答应
了。

到了星期四，我很有纪律，行动也特别快捷。

第一次排球练习，准时报到。先是跟着教练做暖
身操，接着就开始学习排球的各种技巧，如开
球，杀球等等。

″同学，今天我们要选出十二位排球校际代表。
沒有选中的，希望大家继续加油，保持不断练
习，不断挑战的精神。被选中的，你们将会进行
密集训练，因为两个月后的今天，就是校际比赛
的开始。大家明白吗？″教练说。

″明白!″同学回应。

″清楚吗？同学？″

″清楚!″同学再次明确的回答。

"好，同学们，我们先从开球选出两位开球高手代表。大家先自行发球十分钟，时间到，听到吹哨声，就列队，逐一开球。清楚吗？"教练发出第一条指示。

"清楚！"同学们答道。

对我，被选中校际代表从来不是我的目标，一开始就是纯好玩，不必呆在家，无聊透顶。但是，开球对我绝对是一大挑战，因为不曾成功把球发过网，开到对方那一端。但是，为了听从教练指示，维护运动员的纪律，我还是硬着头皮参与，跟着大伙儿列队轮流开球。

轮到我时，我全神贯注，拿出当年幼稚园串珠比赛的专注卯足全身之力，啪！

"哇！终于过网了！"全场哗然，大家拍手叫好。

然而，我没有因为第一次开过网而开心，反而莫名其妙的沮丧。同学的喝彩，好像尖锐的针扎在我幼小心灵。

这负面情绪，我当时没有流露出来，但它却在我的运动生涯扎下毒针似的。从此，我就是与球类运动绝缘，甚至任何超过一个人的运动都不想碰，任何要竞争，要对擂的运动项目我都保护距离。

当时，一个人有三次开球机会，我第一次，也是唯一一次发球成功，接下来的二次预料中败北，结果可想而知，我出局了。

我依然跟着姐姐和校队到处去比赛，不是代表，不是后补，倒是开心的当起了单人啦啦队，重点就是跟车，跟队，跟风和出来玩玩讨开心罢了。

小学五年级那一年，随着姐姐升上中学而因此结束了排球练习。其实也结束了我对任何球类或运动的兴趣和练习。除非学校休育课必修，否则我是运动绝缘体。

我要学鋼琴

难得学校假期，且碰到爸爸晚上沒约见任何客户介绍人寿保单。所以，爸爸晚饭后七点半就载我去当时最大的购物广场逛街，顺便等妈妈九点下班。

哇！小时候的我们，不只三餐都只在家吃，从来沒有上过餐厅用餐之外，连逛街也是一种奢侈。所以，当爸爸说今晚早点去载妈妈时，这种言语所不能形容的喜悦时刻，绝对毕生难忘，千载难逢。

更开心的是，见到妈妈时，她竟然忙里偷闲，带我去逛街。原来，让爸爸提早带我来是妈妈的意思，因为广场这周末有举办鋼琴表演会，妈妈想让我见识见识。

我站在那里，欣赏着哥哥姐姐们双手在琴键上优雅自如地弹出悠美的音乐，仿佛全世界好像停留在我眼前，感觉自己随着音符，展翅忘我，遨游在这美妙动听的鋼琴旋律中。

"小妹，走了，妈妈要下班回家了。" 妈妈的话似乎被鋼琴声淹没了，我完全沉醉其中没听见她的叫唤。

"小妹! 我们要回家了!" 这次是爸爸的声音。我有听到，但依然没反应，依然自我陶醉中。

"小妹! 我们走了!" 这次是妈妈说完话，也不管三七二十一，就把我连根拔起，拖走了。

她一边拖，我一边扯。小学四年级的我，与大人斗力气，岂能有胜算呢？此时，我灵机一动，使出放声大哭的法宝，加上讲道理，苦苦哀求，希望慈祥的妈妈会心动。

"妈，我要学弹琴，求求你，我要学弹琴，我真的很喜欢，我答应你我一定会好好学习的。。。" 就这样重复的哀求，妈妈果然心动了。

我们又重返表演会的现场。负责老师似乎也观察到我的坚持和妈妈的无奈，马上走前来，邀请我们坐下。

"亲爱的家长，现在报名有优惠，免注册费，也不用急着买鋼琴，还会送初学者琴谱一本，此优惠只限这周末现场报名的学生！小孩学鋼琴好处多多，双手运用有助左右脑发展，更可陶冶性情。。。" 老师真的很用心的给爸妈做招生讲解。站在一旁的我，是很了解妈妈的无奈，因为家里收支入不敷出，学鋼琴简直就是奢侈；但是，我真的真的很喜欢。

"好吧！一个月二十五零吉，我们先缴。下周六，正式上第一堂鋼琴课。" 天下父母心，省吃俭用，都是为了子女。

我也沒辜负众望，第一级考到特优，还被老师选去参加学校年终合唱团表演，更一度获得钢琴双重合奏的表演机会，最后也完成英国皇家音乐学院第八级乐理和钢琴弹奏资格。

虽然我高中三毕业后，有意想继续到英国皇家音乐学院修音乐系，默想自己在国际舞台上当交响乐团总指挥的豪迈和专业。但是，自己既不是音乐资优生，鋼琴技艺也无法为我取得全额奖学金或保送计划等，贷款自费的路又很漫长。所以一切的梦想，在黎明划破黑夜之际，又回到一如往常的现实。

捨不得

很快的就来到小学五年级，我就读的五甲班。

当时的华文小学检定考试是在五年级进行。考获四个 A 或以上，可申请直接就读中学一年级，省略多读一年的小学六年级。这所谓的"跳级生"所带来的效应，无非就是看到班上很多家庭有经济能力的同学去课外补习，当然少不了各科老师在校给额外的练习题和不断的温习。

我无限感激老师们的付出，他们不只把我们教会教懂，还重复给我们温习和做历届考题等等，确保大家成绩榜首，学业有成。老师这种负责到底的精神和态度，给我做人处事立下很好的基础和榜样，更让我欣慰没有能力上补习班也不是一件丢脸或输定的事。

谢谢老师们。您们教，我用心学，认真多做，我相信我一样行！这是我那时候的默想。

哇！成绩放榜了！

我们一早就冲去学校。老师一个个发成绩单。紧张又兴奋，想看又担心。偷偷看，一个 A，两个 A，三个 A，四个 A，共四个 A 加两个 B。我很满意了，我有资格当"跳级生"，啦。。啦。。啦啦啦啦。

奇怪的是，这时候我的小小心灵有莫名奇妙的挣扎，拼了整一年，凭个人实力考到了，怎么却对申请"跳级生"这事踌躇不前了呢？这不就是我梦寐以求的吗？

一会儿自认不是五 A 或全科六 A 生，跳上去会不会赶不上初一新生？一会儿又担心爸爸经济负担又要加重了；一会儿又到处问同学"跳"到那个中学；一会儿又担心自己太幼稚，深怕心智不成熟，见到中学的哥哥姐姐们，会不会被欺负？

好啦！脑子里的千万个为什么总算告一段落！

我做了最后决定，即不申请任何中学。免得沒中选又伤心，中选又捨不得小学的老师和同学们。

所以，我决定与他们共渡小学六年级，这一年的美好时光。

对啦! 我决定了! 就是舍不得同窗五年，有些甚至六年(含幼稚园一年)的朋友, 舍不得教我爱我的老师们，舍不得错过拍摄六年级全级和班级毕业照，舍不得这么快长大。

说也奇怪，因舍不得而决定留下，带给我非笔墨所能形容的平安和喜乐。我在默想中微笑着，无限感恩眼前拥有的一切。

全级第一名

谢谢我们的鄰居，她一身奉献给华文教育，终身在华小执教，维护华教。当年，是她来我们家告诉我爸爸说小孩一定要继续读华校，再辛苦也要维护华教，这精神一定要传承。。。

所以，姐姐、弟弟和我就这样继续就读华文中学。

由于这独立华文中学距离我们家有约 20 公哩路，我们早上六点十五分一定要走出去等校车，要不然七点到不了学校。下午一时三十分下课就要冲出校门，十分钟后校车就开走了，下午二时三十分到四十分才会到家。

早餐就是十年如一日的面包涂牛油咖椰(Kaya,椰浆鸡蛋制成的甜浆)，午餐两，三点才回家吃。胃病就是在那时候熬出来的。零用钱也顶多马币一零吉，还要收好，因为每周有三个下午要留下来。两个下午是额外补习以马来文为媒介语的国家检定考试(初中三的 SRP 和 高中二的 SPM)，；另一个下午是学校规定每个学生都要任选一项课外活动。

我清楚记得，自己零用钱非常有限，所以只能点干捞面 kosong（kosong 就是不加料），因为加料就超出预算了。

即便种种来回学校的不便利，加上三餐不定时的困扰和非常有限的零用钱，还是动摇不了我求学的欲望。上了中学的我，顿时开窍，一班五十八人也不影响我专心听课，没有补习也不延误我的学习和理解。迟回家，有胃病也阻挡不了我的晚自习和完善作业。最感恩的是，我的记忆力，虽然没有"一目十行"的功力，似乎也到了"过目不忘"的境界。

我默想自己可以得第一名，默想自己登台领奖的成就感。就这样，我的认真，真正又成效了。不只全班第一名，还以总平均 90.17 分，获得全级第一名。

谢谢当小学教师的邻居之启蒙，谢谢父母的支持，谢谢中学老师依然专业又用心，最开心莫过于一群幼稚园和小学的知己朋友还是同班，同校，我好喜欢这个有科学实验室，电脑室的中学，我感恩自已不负众望，名列前茅，学有所成。

爷爷走了

一眨眼，就渡过了五年的中学生涯，来到了中学最后一年的高中三年级。

这一年也是我们家非常煎熬的一年，因为爷爷病倒了。

爷爷在第二次世界大战前，约 1938 年左右，从中国随他小叔南下，飘洋过海来到古晋谋生。爷爷的爸爸在他三岁时就英年早逝，独生子的他，出生于广东省汕头市，因为家庭清寒赤贫，爷爷的小学一年级是在古晋华小就读的，当初他是班上最年长的插班生，年龄十七岁。听爷爷说，他也读了两年小学而已，因为要协助他小叔干活，尽快赚足够的船费让他妈妈，也是我的曾祖母可以越洋过来团聚。

爷爷一生劳碌，早期在老巴刹(俗称菜市场)摆摊卖木薯，地瓜。芋头等，收入微薄，可也养活三个儿子，四个女儿的大家庭。爷爷奶奶一直与我们同住，让我从小见证家有一老，如有一宝的温暖。我有太多与爷爷的美好回忆。

从小，爷爷是我的活鬧钟，是他叫醒我。我还限制爷爷不可以开门进来叫我，也不可以大声敲门吓醒我。因此，爷爷用心的走到外面，从窗口轻声叫醒我，十年如一日。

爷爷也是我的忠实守卫，每天早上，都是他领着我们到路口等校车，回来时，远远就可看到爷爷撑伞等我们回来了，风雨无阻，就是要確保我们路上安全。

我自认爷爷最疼我，尽管他对子孙们也疼爱有加。也许我是他最忠实的听众，又有着不耻下问的精神，爷爷只给我讲，重复地讲他的童年往事，成家立业的辛酸，二战的民不聊生等等。每每看到他讲得沉醉在往事里，我也仿佛与他共乘时光机回到从前。

我个人觉得最经典的辛酸史莫过于爷爷读了小学
二年级之后就辍学，为了就是干活存钱让曾祖母
早日来到古晋一事。

当时爷爷干的粗活是帮建筑工地扛盖房子砌砖用
的大砖块。薪酬以砖块数量计费，条件就是完好
无损的把砖块从码头扛到好几公里外的工地。

爷爷为了在最短时间内尽快让他妈妈南下古晋，常常超负荷，多扛几块砖。原因很简单，路程一样，只有多扛几块才赚越多，又因路程遥远，日出而作，日落而息，除了多扛才能多赚，别无他法。但步行路上，偶尔被爷爷的小叔"逮"到了他严重超负荷，命令爷爷先把几块卸在路边。爷爷是很激动的搏斗，但也无耐的顺服了。说到这里，爷爷看着我说："你看爷爷长不高，又严重驼背就是当初压出来的。小叔为我好，担心压坏身体，不会生，没有后代。。。"

爷爷天生劳碌命，退休了还是闲不下来。其实是有高血压了，但从没透露身体状况，每天依然在后院斩草清理。

至到有一天，爷爷没叫醒我，我去他房间，才发现爷爷左嘴唇冒出很多白沫，无法言语，也坐不起来。"爸!!不好了!!快点叫救护车。。。"我喊着冲出房间。

原来，爷爷严重中风了。左边全部瘫痪了。在医院住了整一个月，当时，外公也因老人病先后入院，且床位左右相望，方便家属同时照料。这真是家里的艰难时期，永远的惨痛回忆。

当爷爷情况稳定时，医生只建议让他回家安享晚年。这时的爷爷，脑袋是清晰的，但由于严重中风，无法言语表达，只剩眼神交流和右边肢体语言。

我当初就读高中三理科班。全国独中统一考试的成绩就是决定未来升学的关键，我自认在照料爷爷这块，愧疚没尽太大的孝心，倒是天天轮到我讲故事给爷爷听，间接帮奶奶，父母完善部分家务事而已。

同一年，在家相聚了几个月，爷爷似乎不要拖累照顾他的人，有一天就静静的离开人间了。从此，我的活闹钟停摆了，门卫也寿终正寝了，讲古说故事也正式落幕，无法再重来。

我哭了很久，但只能默想爷爷在天之灵，给我力量作最后冲击，考到最好成绩，圆了我出国深造之梦，鹏程万里，回报最疼我的爷爷，但我来不及回报，爷爷就走了。

算命看未来

高中三统考放榜了!!!哇！我考获五 A 四 B。虽然成绩不如默想中的理想，但也不是差强人意。

由于是理科班，一班四十三人，几乎每个人在成绩放榜之后，都忙着向世界各地的大学提出申请，准备出国深造。其实，统考之前，同学们已经积极出席校内、校外举办的各种教育展。

班上同学的升学之路，比比皆是，主要是高三统考文平相当于多国大学的基础班水准，符合大部分大学入学资格，所以，感觉条条大路通罗马。

有远至美国，加拿大的，也有去英国，苏格兰的，当然也少不了去纽西兰，澳洲深造的，还有一部份去台湾或在国内先读先修班后衔接到国外继续深造的。

大家都胸有成竹，信心满满，各奔前程。

虽然我已经从小小心灵成长为青春少女的清纯，

但面对当时人生一大里程碑，我依旧茫然。即便我默想自己圆出国深造的美梦，但这个默想所要付出的行动和举措，似乎是我茫然的主要因素，因为它太遥远，太超出我青春少女的思维和能力。

看到班上同学，一个个出国，还有拍不完的机场顺风送行团体照，我从麻木不仁渐渐感到惊慌失措。我不能像小学的天真与无知，也无法用哭闹逼迫父母给我学弹钢琴的招式要他们给我出国深造。这时的我，认真的守株待兔，等待好时机好心情时，腼腆的向爸爸开口：

"爸，高中统考之后可以出国读书吗？"，

爸爸顿了许久，望着我说："小妹，爸爸只能供你到中学毕业，没有准备预算让你读大学。"

我点了点头，掉头就上楼回房去了。一边走，一边眼泪不听使唤的流下，不敢用手擦拭，深怕家人看到我失望茫然的样子。

出国深造的梦想真的破碎了吗？爸爸没预算，我就不能想办法吗？自小，我的默想一定心想事成，美梦成真，怎么可能到了 18 岁就无法发挥功效呢？不可能。路是人走出来的，天无不绝人之路。

默想中，想到姐姐读台湾师范大学是中学校董保送，也就是说学杂费全津贴，条件是毕业后回校服务五年。我也喜欢执教，为人师表，桃李满天下，这工作很高尚又有满足感，最重要是咱们家没有读大学的预算，所以，这途径或许是目前唯一最好的出国升学管道。

好吧！我真的去学校拿侨生赴台升学表格填志愿。我非常记得所有台湾的师范大学我都填完了，最后一栏，老师建议我填写-"国立侨生大学先修班"，原因是若无法直接分发大学，起码一定会被派到先修班。其实，老师知道我华文科只有 B，按过去的经验，要直接分发还可能史无前例。

由于台湾新学年第一学期报到落在九月份，而中学统考是在十月分进行。所以，从今年的十一月份成绩放榜到明年九月份才开学，间中就是漫长的等待和无奈。等待台湾侨生委员会捎来好消息，而无奈是因为同班同学一个个出国了，我的前途还是未知数。

等待中，我也帮鄰居的三个小孩补习全科，赚取我学汽车和考执照的费用。剩余的时间和储蓄，我也偷偷去报考托福，希望自己的英文可达到西方英国大学入学资格的英文水平。以此同时，也自费把英国皇家音乐学院的鋼琴第八级考完。因为我从小就最想去英国皇家音乐学院读音乐系，专攻指挥官认证。无耐托福成绩出炉后也是普通而不达标，鋼琴第八级也只是"及格"罢了.

当留学英国梦确定破碎了，赴台升学的成绩又迟迟未揭晓时，我在这人生低谷期，竟然跟幼稚园兼小学同班，中学同校的老知己相约去相命预知未来。

无奈这段时间做的事情都是偷偷摸摸的，主要是不让爸妈因无能力送小孩出国深造而愧疚，同时自己也要积极想办法圆梦。
那天下午，与老朋友去见了那位号称很灵很精准的算命师，他看到我们也吓了一跳，乳臭未干，沒见过市面，来算什么命？！！

"请问你们有何事相求?"

"我可以为你们做什么？"

可是，我们就是死赖不走。

最终我们的坚持打动了这位老先生，他也只好要了我们的生辰八字之后，反复翻阅他的"算命辞典"，足足耗了一个下午，每人各写了整整一页红色纸张的命定和预言。

感恩那天下午，沒有其他算命"顧客"排队等待，要不然肯定恨死我们這两个丫头。这算命师最终归纳了我的命是"富贵命"，尤其晚年，多子多孙等等。。反正当时是让我更茫然无奈，因为与我现实状况，简直就是天渊之别，但也不否认听了有点"暗爽"，自我安慰一下。

老先生也给我改个同音别字的名 -"娅瑧"，要我天天用，天天写。但是这事后来被爸爸发觉，痛骂了一顿。

"真真是爸爸给你取的名，凡事相信自己，靠自己做到最好。算啥么命？没奋斗，没努力，算了命会马上变好吗？。。。"

赴台升学结果出炉了，我没有富贵命的惊喜，反正就是被老师说中了。。。对。。就是中了最后志愿。。国立侨生大学先修班。

事到如今，尘埃落定，我还是以感恩的心，谢谢默想出国深造成事，即便不是心中想去的国家，更不是想唸的学校或科系。

就这样，隔年的九月份就出国了。。。

填志愿

感谢亲朋戚友的红包和祝福，妈妈说总算筹足了飞往台湾的单程机票，至于多余的生活费就无能为力了。我安慰妈妈说："不要紧，姐姐在那儿有工读，她有存些钱等着我，妈妈，请放心！。"

终于到了启程的日子，由于是九月份了，也沒有同学来送行拍顺风团体照，因为大家都出国了。不过，我们还有八、九个同班同学同一班机，并不感觉孤单。

抵台后，旅台同学会热情接机，并安顿我们在宿舍休息过一夜。就寝前，大家先到会议室聚会，听讲解，顺便收取新生的马币以便协助兑换成台币。

"这位同学，你是不是少给了？怎么这么少？那里夠用？"

那位学长在十几二十人面前，大声地向我询问。

那时候的我，多想找个洞钻进去。我身上确实没有多余的马币，但是这问题真的问得没错，可也狠狠的在我伤口上撒盐。

"学长，对的，因为大部分台币在我姐姐那儿。"

这句话，我本来只是用来安抚妈妈的，沒想到来到异国他乡，还要重复用上。差别之处，这时候是安抚我为了出国深造，青春无悔的心，而更主要它还是个让我得以下台的美丽谎言，不让无知的外来因素击败我的信心与盼望。

隔天，新生被送往各自的学校，姐姐也陪我一起过去。由于预算真的非常有限，我只买了台币290的棉被，薄到冬天摄氏七，八度时，我还得穿着在夜市买的，也是台币290的寒衣，才勉强熬过冬天，而且还撑过大学四年。一个20公斤大行李箱，连衣架，洗衣塊都从古晋带过来，大学毕业时，也是同一个20公斤大行李箱回去，没有超重，也没有浪费。

在这一年，让我窝心的事有二：一个是被选中女宿舍总楼长，另一个是有机会在校园工读，刚好赚取足够之包含住宿和伙食的学杂费。

我选读甲组工程科,组内共 200 多位来自世界各地的侨生。第一学期,发奋图强的结果是排名第13。可是,到了第二学期,也就是先修班的总排名,有点退步,只得 31 名。这也意谓我是第 31 的顺位选取甲组各大学科系的学生。

一大早,我就按名次排队,内心是忐忑不安的,因为一个人只有三分钟的时间,在佈满 200 多个各校学系的大字报前,选一个学系而已。所以,手上的志愿是要预先准备好的,要不然选不到自己想要的科系,就真的慌得手忙脚乱,不知所措了。

完了!第 25 名选了我的第一志愿。因为我们就在课室旁边列队,挨着墙,顶着窗口,还是可以清楚偷听到里边的话语。我不停默想第 26 名到第 30 名不要选中我的第二志愿,要不然,我真的慌了。因为,我冒汗的手掌心只写了三个志愿。

感恩。轮到我时，不假思索，就按下去的。

对！就是填了工业工程与管理学系。

我选了国立大学，学杂费是私立大学的三分之一。听学长姐说学杂费和生活费是可以靠工读凑齐的，选了个比较有趣，不太专精的工程系，主要也是让自己趁学习之余有较多时间打工凑学杂费。

工读生

我的大学生涯，除了读书和考获大学学位以外，就是打工赚取生活费和学杂费了。

一年共两个学期，每学期约四个月，第一学期是九月开课，第二学期是二月开课。由于我选读工业工程与管理学系，共四年的工程学士学位，所以，我上课时只利用课余时间打工，赚取生活费。寒暑假就全职打工，赚取两学期学杂费。因此，有了打工计划，有了费用目标，剩下的就是豁出去，采取行动了。

当我在默想自己的打工计划时，灵感告诉我去餐厅打工最实在。因为赚外块之余，伙食也解决了，这应该是最完美的战略呀！

于是，我寻求学长姐的建议后，先到校园停放脚踏车场物色一台必须沾满灰尘又没上锁的代步工具。原因是这里有个不成文的惯例，也就是毕业的学长姐，若无意带走脚踏车，就只把锁带走，留下脚踏车。

顺理成章，过了二个半月的暑假，因为无人认领，脚踏车自然布满灰尘，方便新学年的学弟姐辨认和带走，也是一种爱的传承。一个已经留传了几十载的爱之文化。

我踩着在校园里千挑万选中的二手脚踏车，先从校区内的餐厅开始，一家家看看墙上是否有张贴"招聘工读生"之类的贴条。

第一餐厅，沒有，心想沒有也好，因为它靠近男宿舍。

第二餐厅一樓，沒有。来到二樓，也沒有。不行，要硬着头皮问老板娘了，因为第二餐厅靠近女宿舍。

"老板娘，请问您缺工读生打菜吗？"

"午餐时间，你可以吗？上午 11 点到下午 1 点左右。就打菜给买经济杂饭的学生，下班后可以免费自选一肉二菜，打包饭盒回宿舍。"老板娘说道。

"好!好!可以，请问几时可以开始？"我不假思索的回答。

" 明天开始。周一到周五。"老板娘直接了当回答。

"好!好!明天见!谢谢老板娘。"我心中感恩午餐有着落了。

我继续骑着铁马到校外的餐馆，这回主要找含晚餐的工读机会。

走着走着，看到了!太兴奋了。一切都非常顺心顺意。前面一家台式餐馆正"寻找工读生"。走进去，刚好老板娘在。

"老板娘，请问您还需求工读生吗？"我很客气的问道。

"是你本人吗？主要是端菜上桌和打扫，可以吗？"老板娘回答道。

"可以!可以!请问上班时间是几点到几点？

"我们晚餐比较多人，所以请你下午五点就来上班，我们师父亲自下厨先煮给大家吃，一般上客人六点左右就陆续前来，忙到九点左右，收拾打扫完才可离开。"老板娘仔细的解释。

"好的!好的!请问我几时可以上班？"听到晚餐又有着落了，时间又不影响上课，我不管三七二十一，就大胆答应了。

"明天可以来上班了。"老板娘简单一句话带过。

"好的!好的!明天下午五点准时打卡，谢谢老板娘。"我兴奋得猛点头道谢，跟着手舞足蹈的离开。

就这样，我每天的午餐和晚餐就解决了，还有收入供早餐和其他开销。

暑假来临前，也在校旁公寓底楼的小超市找到收银员的暑假工读机会，时间是下午四点到凌晨十二点关门。这也是因为那餐厅老板娘在餐饮业奋斗了整二十载，奉献了无数的周末和假期，她最终决定不做了，要结业休息享乐去了。所以我也只好上 BBS 网再搜索新的打工机会。

也因为是暑假，不用上课，所以我默想要善用假期的每段空档。果真皇天不负有心人，因为本地生和经济有能力的留台生多半暑假回家，所以校园附近的工读机会就是一大把。

感恩的我，早上找到两份补习，一份是帮一个小学男孩暑假一对一恶补全科，另一份是一个小学女孩暑假在家一对一学钢琴，因为有兴趣了，开学才去找专业钢琴老师学习。

就这样，我暑假基本上就只剩下午两点到四点可以午休，看看书，写写信回家，洗个澡又要去小超市当收银员了。

四年的大学生活，真的因为当了工读生，充满了无限美好回忆。

间中也有晚上到住家里给一对情侣教授英语会话，最后还被邀请参加他们俩的结婚晚宴，那也是我来台后第一次参加的婚宴，真正大开眼界，间中，也曾帮一名单亲妈妈在她出差美国的十天里，照顾她幼儿园的独生女，当时就暂住她家，负责小朋友的三餐，就寝和载送等。另外，还帮教授做文书处理工作，把文章以中文输入归檔；也有在校内侨委会办公室工读，更有在晚上去高级餐厅弹奏鋼琴等等。

这四年的大学生活虽然很辛苦的自给自足，但绝对过得充实和踏实。这个"社会大学"的工读经验，为我未来的全职奠定了更扎实的待人处事礼仪和工作态度。

算一算，我在台共呆了快五年，侨大先修班一年加大学四年。数一数，这五年来，我只给父母要了至多马币五千元。那就是第一次来台的单程机票，约马币两千加上第一学期的学杂费和部分开销，约三千马币而已。之后的学杂费，包括回国机票都是工读赚来的。

9 比 1 的珍贵

女生在以理工科系为主的大学就读，就是有这个优势。尤其我就读的大学。男生与女生的比例是九比一。这可真是乐透了。

在台湾，很流行联谊活动，就是社团或系所间的男生会举办"爬地"，然后派传单，一对一邀请其他系的女生参加，达到联合举办活动和增进友谊的目的。

我最记得，也值得一提的联谊活动就是"夜间观看萤火虫"。首先是男生一对一邀请女生，当天晚上，先邀请女方共进晚餐，比较节俭或含蓄的男生就会先外带香鸡排和烧仙草后才去宿舍载女同学。大学都是骑机车(摩托车)的，有 50cc 的小绵羊，也有 150cc 的中型机车。

晚上八点正，后面校门口挤满一台台机车，全是男女一对。到齐了，大家就浩浩荡荡往小山丘开去。到了目的地，大家把车灯一熄，哗！天上的星星会说话，地上的男女都牵手。走了一段路后，迎面而来的就是一大片空旷的草地，清楚看到草地旁的丛林佈满一闪一闪亮晶晶的萤火虫，好像天上放光明，满地都是小星星。

我还有些忘不了"被追"罗曼蒂克史。这里就挑几个有感动，印象深刻的来回味那种"九比一"的珍贵，好像掌上明珠般的疼爱。

由于我除了上课，就是打工。说真的，沒时间"被追"，更沒闲暇谈恋爱。所以，喜欢我的男生，也很用心。

记得在第一个冬季，因为沒钱回家过年，所以和另一位侨生去面包店打工，这个仰慕者，还真的天天来探班，每晚帮我们关店，走路陪我们回宿舍去，再出来吃宵夜聊天。

还有一回我因为打工忘了吃饭，回到宿舍后因胃病发作而昏厥倒地。刚好另一班的高材生，在那一刻突然想打电话找我聊天，发现我情况不对，必须马上送医。在室友的协助下，我就这样伏在他的背上，让他用机车火速把我送到附近医院看诊打点滴。过程细节我真的记不得了，但迷迷糊糊中，我还是清楚听到一路上他不断地说："抱紧我，快到了!"

当我苏醒后，睁开双眼见到病床旁的第一个人，就是这位高材生，旁边的粥也是他特地出去外带回来。他无私的关爱，我是一辈子感恩。之后，为了到他家乡作客，我还省吃俭用，挪用了工读赚来的学杂费跟他回乡，也是答谢他一直以来的关照。无奈我归心似箭，所以异国婚姻从来没有在我的"爱情字典"里，也动摇不了我的初心。

还有一位学长，知道我在特定的晚上都会去运动场跑步健身，他也会专程前往再制造偶遇；知道我有胃病，不定时买宵夜给我，示爱之举更不在话下了。可惜我似乎铁石心肠，始终也没动情。

话说大四毕业了，全班同学有组团去环岛旅行。其中有一个同班男同学，还在某个海滩扛了一大包沙上车，夜夜熬夜筛选"星"沙，大家都不知道他用意何在，也有同学猜测他的意中人究竟是谁。当七天的环岛结束后，大家都拖着疲惫但愉悦的心情回到宿舍后不久，我竟然接到这位扛了一大包沙的男同学来电。

"喂，真真吗？请问今晚可以请你吃个饭吗？"男同学客气但诚恳的说道。

"好呀，请问几点？在宿舍门口等你，对吗？"

"待会傍晚六点半，对，在女宿舍门口，不见不散。拜拜啦！。"对方兴高采烈地掛线了。

原来熬夜一周，制作出这一小瓶天然星型沙粒的就是要送给我。

"原来你是要送给我？可是。。我下周就回古晋了。你们还要继续选修硕士学位。不能担误你的大好前途。"我快人快语的表态。

"沒关系，你收下。这是我的小小心意，也是我的真情表白，希望你回去之后，彼此保持联系，哪天想念台湾了，欢迎你随时回来，我家管吃管住，只要你想回来。。。"男同学含蓄的说道。

"一定，一定保持联系。谢谢你的星沙，我会永远带在身边。"我还真的说到做到，尽管搬了几次家，我还是收藏到今天，唯一没有兑现的就是回台相聚，当然这段情谊也仅仅停留在星沙的浪漫，没有进一步发展下去。

隔天，另一位班上男同学也是邀请我吃晚餐饯行，因为我就快离台回乡了。

"真真，饭后你有趕时间回去吗？"这位男同学问到。

"还好，行李就一大箱而已，收拾完了。"我简单带过。

"那你后天回去，我可以载你去机场。"他诚心提出爱的最后邀约。

"沒事，我之前工读的小超商店主己经说好载我上机场了，谢谢你啦！"

"不用担心，我们会再见。你硕士毕业时，我一定回来参加你们的毕业典礼" 我很认真的回答道。

"这样，反正时间还早，就让我尽地主之余，载你去遊车河，向新竹说再见。好吗？"

"好呀！太好了!先谢谢啦。不客气了。"

其实这男同学志在带我回他新竹市的家作客，除了介绍我给他母亲之外，还介绍他住家给我，很诚恳的说家里万事俱备，只欠个女主人。

顿时，一股忘我的被爱感，让我沉醉在幸福美满的幻觉，久久回神不过来。但理智的我，"清醒"过来后,嘴角冒出一句坚定的话来："嗯。。哈哈哈哈。。。我要回古晋了。。祝福你硕士学有所成，鹏程万里。"

就这样，一个又一个，数不尽的男追女珍贵史就随着我回到古晋，而成为心中永远珍藏的回忆了。

同学，别汇了!

大学的宿舍是四人一房，左右各有上下铺。很感恩的是，大学第三和第四年时，我的其中一名室友也是我的同班同学。谢谢校方这么用心的安排，让我感受到同学互相照应的温暖。

那一年的暑假，本来按部就班工读来凑下一学年两个学期的学杂费是绝对万无一失的完美安排。可是，我就是因为"九比一的珍贵"，答应了那位救命恩人，一定要亲自到访澳门，答谢那位高材生而让我下一学年的第二学期学杂费，在缴学费期限内依然无法凑足。

大三那一年，我的姐姐也已毕业回古晋执教了。我的弟弟又刚来台湾读大学一年级。所以，我绝不可能向家里要钱，况且，从来台之后，都不曾向家里要过一分一毫的生活费或学杂费。

"婷，这学期的学杂费，你可以先帮我缴吗？我分三个月，每次月底收到工读金后就转进你户口，可以吗？"无计可施的之下，我只好向即是室友，又是同学的她开口了。

"沒问题，不要这样客气啦！你平时读书之余，还要工读，辛苦了，我帮你垫学期学费，没关系啦！我爸每个月给我很多零用钱，我也没什么花费，夠的。"婷慷慨解囊还叫我不用还她哩！

"不行!不行! 有借有还，这是我的信用，也是我做人的原则。要不然，我们天天见面，我看到你，我也不好意思啦！" 我迫不及待回答。

"嗯！好吧！我真的不介意，就顺你意思吧！"

"我现在马上转帐到学校指定银行户口，列明你的学号，月底，你方便才转帐给我，不急噢！真的不急。"婷客气的说。

"好的！好的！谢谢啦。有你真好。。。"我感恩的说道。

一眨眼，月底就到了，我信守承诺的转了三分之一的帐款到婷的戶口。接下来的日子，尤其周末没去校园餐厅工读时，三餐就是一条芋头面包，早餐两片，午餐和晚餐各四片。有时就吃饼干而已。

反正，到最后，搞到营养不良，时不时蹲下去再站起来时，就 天旋地转、眼冒金星、目眩头晕的。

但是，为了坚持我做人的原则，人可穷，不可没志气。第二个月底，我如常把另外的三分之一余额转到婷的戶口里。心中也沾沾自喜，因为只剩最后的三分之一，再坚持多一个月就可恢复正常的饮食。

"真。。我爸爸有话给你说。。。。" 婷很委屈的边说边把宿舍分机拿给我。

"什么？你爸要骂我向你借錢，迟迟不还？！！" 我脸青发白，一副自知理亏的样子。

"不是啦！不是啦！我给他说了，他硬要给你本人解释，没事，没事，你就接个电话吧！拜托啦"婷反倒恳求我配合她。

我双手颤抖，脑袋一片空白。因为之前跟室友闲聊时，婷曾说过，她家里当军人的爸爸若是说一，无人敢说二。她还曾经说过她爸爸也不允许她出外工读，目的是要她专心读书，考上硕士班。

"伯父，您好。。我是真真。。婷的室友。。伯父找我有什么事吗？"我结结巴巴、轻声问道。

"同学，伯父看到婷户口有錢进帐，追问之下，又不是工读赚来，又不是什么奖励金。原来是你汇钱给她。。。"另一端传来丹田有力的话语。

"对不起，伯父，是我先让婷帮忙缴学费，但是，我答应她分三个月付清，还有最后一个月，不好意思。。。伯父。。不好意思。。。"我打断伯父的会话，说到眼泪都快要不听使唤了。

"同学，伯父不是这个意思。"

"同学，伯父请你不要再汇钱。"

"同学，伯父知道侨生，出国留学已经很辛苦了，不要再汇了，最后一个月不用再汇了，伯父今天给你打电话，就是要亲口告诉你不用再汇了，当成伯父给你的，好吗？。"伯父一口气交待来电的用意。

"谢谢伯父，谢谢伯父，对不起误会您了。谢谢伯父。。。"这时的我，除了感恩谢意道不尽，顿时脑袋真的沒有其他词彙了。

真的，出国深造，这默想成真中，一路走来，是由多少恩人，贵人相助呀! 我何时才能报答。

另一个同班同学，也是我的恩人之一。他把他的50cc "小绵羊"机车借给我，以方便我到距离校区较远的地方工读。虽然他说他要换台 150cc 的机车，但他其实可以变卖这台小绵羊，然后用更少的现金买台新的。可是，他只是说不急，我先用着。

感恩在借用期间也从来没零件耗损或机身有故障。我还记得大四毕业归还小绵羊给他后，他就卖掉了。这位同学实际的帮助，是我一辈子都无法回报的。

大学毕业了

大年四年，就在用心学习和勤奋工读之间来到了最后一个学期了。

我记得非常清楚班上有 52 个人，就 50 个台湾本籍加两个侨生，一个来自澳门，一个就是我，来自古晋。

同学们除了忙于筹划班上毕业旅行之外，也商讨谁能成为班上代表上台领取本科毕业证书。由于每年校内整两千名毕业生，来自本科，硕士，博士等，所以校方规定本科只能一班一名代表上台领全班毕业证书，硕、博士才有机会一个个上台领各自的毕业证书。

那时候，我是班上第七名，总平均八十几分以上。当时的直升硕士规定是一班只给本科成绩前十名的学生，其余就得通过硕士笔试检定等繁琐程序。还有，若前十名的其中一位无兴趣直升，考获第十一名的学生就可自动直升硕士，豁免笔试。

我当初归心似箭，即便考获班上第七名，有直升硕士的资格，但还是放弃这机会，让给第十一名同学。

"佑，我有件事给你说"。我主动摇个电话给第十一名的男同学。

"真，请说。有什么事我可以帮忙？"对方传来有同学关爱的语气。

"是这样的，你也知道我可以直升硕士，但我真的想回家了，先打工赚钱，帮补家用，因为弟弟才刚完成大一，明年上大二，又是私立大学，学杂费都比我们国立多出两倍，况且我奶奶也年迈了，真的很想回去陪陪她"。

"还有，读了硕士回国，台湾文凭也不受马来西亚承认。"我继续说道："我己经很满足，圆了出国深造的梦想，这四，五年来也谢谢同学们给我的关照"。

我继续说："所以，我今天拨电话给你，是想给你说，你可以代我直升硕士，因为你在班上考获第十一名，不要浪费系所规定的十个名额吧！我答应你，两年后一定来参加你的硕士毕业典礼，好吗？"

"真的吗？哇！这真的是喜哀参半。喜的是，我真心真正感谢真真给我这直升的机会，谢谢！谢谢！我毕身难忘。哀伤的是，我们就要暂时离别了，你两年后，一定要回来探访我们噢！"佑说道。

"一定，一言为定。加油。再见"。我诚恳的说道。

话说同学干部正在商讨谁应该代表班上代领全班毕业证的事宜。听说他们讨论了很久之后，最终达成协议，并派班代给我打电话。

"真真，我们同学决定了"。班代说。

"决定了什么事？有什么我回国前还可以服务大家吗？"我礼貌的回应。

"是这样，班上同学一致通过，委派你作为我们班的代表上台领取毕业证书"。班代直接了当表态。

"不行，不行，我沒资格。我即不是班上第一名，又不是获得杰出优良表现的学生，我只是本年度本科毕业特刊的总召集人而已"。我拒绝了。

"你听我说，听我说。。这绝对是大家的意願。因为班上 52 个人，48 位己决定修读硕士，换句话说，他们都有机会一个个上台领各自的硕士毕业证书。。"班代还沒说完，就被我打断。

"可是，除了我之后，还有另外三位同学，沒修读硕士，又是本地生，我反正要回去了，沒关系啦！我不好意思。。"这时，轮到班代不等我说完，直接插嘴了。

"所以，所以大家派我来给你传答这个讯息。我和你，还有另外两名女同学，我们四个人当中，你成绩最优秀，而且你又要先回马来西亚了，这样，让你代表大家，意义重大。况且，我们三个人是一致举手同意选你的"。

"还有，还有，同学担心你以为大家偏袒你，怀疑黑箱操作，所以推选我，亲自亲口给你捎来这个消息，你真的实至名归，就是你啦！"班代重复道。

"嗯，这真是我回去前，最好的礼物。我爸爸也特地飞过来参加我的毕业典礼，这样，他也感到欣慰，说不定，也为我感到骄傲"。

"好吧！谢谢大家的肯定，感恩大家对我的厚爱。二年后，我一定来参加大家的硕士毕业典礼"。我开心的接受了同学们的献议。

第一时间，我就跑去大学的侨务委员会所报告这个何等的荣耀，顿时自己又陷入另一个两难。

"噫，这是何等高兴的一件事，为何又愁眉苦脸了？"罗姐不解的问道。

"对,我现在烦恼的就是毕业典礼上需要的那一
套端庄得体的长裙。罗姐,你也知道我平时就T
恤加长裤,方便骑机车工读或踩脚车上课,哪来
的长裙,更别说大方得体,可以登台的长裙,何
况我也完全没有这笔预算。"我轻声说道。

"噢!罗姐本来想在毕业典礼的前一天,把漂亮
的长裙,洗好之后送给你和包包的,你这么说
了,我就给不了你惊喜啦!不过先给你说了,你
也可以放一百个心,不用为衣着担心"。罗姐透
露了秘密。

"真的吗?罗姐真好。谢谢啦!我要如何回报
你?"我兴高采烈的问。

"毕业之后,保持联系,就是最好的回报了"。罗
姐说道。

"好的!好的!一定!一定!,明天见啦!"我开心的道
别。

毕业典礼是晚间举行，场地在户外。一切顺利进行，轮到我们那一班，我穿着全白飘逸的长裙，步伐稳健的上台，从时任台湾教育部长手中，代表全班同学领取毕业证书，还要在台上对着镜头笑一下，拍照留念后才下台。

整个过程至多三十秒，但绝对是我人生里程碑中，非常有份量，意义深远，永记在心的三十秒。

三个星期

出国深造时，也是一个二十公斤行李箱，学业有成，回国时也是同一个二十公斤的行李箱。

唯一的最大差别是出国的行李放满美禄，麦片，衣架，洗衣块等道地美食和日常用品。回国时，是塞满了书籍。

感恩后来一，两年的春节有回家过年，已经搬回来不少书籍了。但遗憾的是，那陪了我四，五载的唯一一件紫色风衣和洗得泛白蓝色薄棉被因此被牺牲割舍，放弃带走。当初我是流着热泪，数夜难眠，陪伴着风衣和棉被，万万不舍，因为隔天一早，要放在侨委会，传承给有需要的学弟学妹们。

就这样，戶口只剩台币 100 元，我悄悄道别了宝岛。

回到家，第一件事莫过于大快朵颐道地美食。那就是叻沙和哥罗面。接下来，就是积极投简历，到处找工作。

由于只想在古晋这小地方服务，可以天天回家，享受家的温暖之余，还可以陪年迈多病的奶奶和久违的父母。因为那年姐姐已嫁到台湾来，弟弟又刚去台湾留学，若我再不自动自发，可以想象爸妈多少缺了个帮手。起码有时候，我可以载奶奶去看病或遊车河，兜兜风。

就因为这样，我也没申请古晋以外的工作。

重启我小时候的默想功力，默想尽快找到心目中理想的公司上班工作，真正学有所成，光宗耀祖。

这种等待的日子，又勾起我中学毕业后等待国外大学分发的那种渡日如年的日子。但这次，我不去算命，也不自怨自艾。反而信心满满，耐心等待，用心投简历，再加上默想，默想面试时要如何应对回答，取得对方的肯定和聘用。

鈴。。鈴。。手机响了，银幕上显示出来的号码不是朋友的，是个陌生号码，定眼一看是古晋区域号的有线电话号码。想想，光天化日打过来，就接吧！

"哈啰，请问是真真吗？"对方用流利的英语问道。

"哈啰，您好。是的。我就是"。我也用英语回答。

"我是矽公司的人力部，明天早上十点，请到河滨饭店大厅，请找我公司罗丝小姐报到，你的面试时间是安排在早上十点十五分钟，请问你可以来面试吗？"对方用英文说道。

"OK！OK！没问题，明天见，谢谢。" 一通电话，让我喜出望外。

隔天早上九点就出发，九点半就到了。所谓早起的鸟儿有虫吃。早到可以把心先安下来，观察四周可以让自己对周边环境较熟悉，进而更有信心。

面试我的是两位职称很高的领导。一位是营运副总裁，一位是营运高级经理。可是，面对他们，我有莫名的信心和态度，对答如流，还带齐所有的大学各科的毕业报告和毕业证等个人资料。

"每一科都有一本四人一组的毕业主题报告？"高级经理问道。

"是的，我们不是只有一个人，一分毕业主题报告而已。我们是每一科都有，且都是团队合作，至少三到四人一组。教授的目的就是要训练我们重视团队精神，为我们步入社会做装备。因为工作都是靠团队"。我解释道。

虽然两位领导是这行业的老前辈，但为人亲切。最主要认同我的学历和能力，了解我的大学素质和成就，要不然，我也不会在回来三个星期就找到一份心目中的工作和很好的薪酬待遇。

"她的大学文凭不受马来西亚认证，我们不能聘请她。。。"人力资源负责人与副总裁的对话，由于语气声调有点激亢，所以，我坐在另一端还是清楚听到。

"沒事，我们不是政府机构，我们是私人机构。只要我承认她的能力，她的态度，她的学历，就可以了。你就给她出聘书吧！下周可以请她直接来报到上班了"。副总裁为我据理力争的对话，也被我听到了。

十五分钟之后。。。

"真真，请到这边来签妳的聘书。签字之前，请详细读取每一个细节，有什么不懂，请发问。若要带回去还是需要更长的时间，也请告之，我可以更改报到日。。。"那个人力资源经理对我说道。

"好的。我现在就看，有疑问再请教您，现在就签，不需要带回去了，谢谢"。我反应也快，深怕带回去，对方是否又有变数了。

五分钟之后。。。

"马丽先生，我都明白了，我也签了，这里有两份。是不是你一份，我一份？"初生牛犊不怕虎的我问道。

"是的，那你八月三日，周一早上八点半到我们办公室报到，地址如聘书所注明。试用期三个月。周休二日，职称和薪酬福利如聘书所述。报到时，请记得携带身份证，我们要为你开银行户口，方便公司月底线上发放薪资等。。"。人力资源经理，似乎标准的台词，一字不漏的解释道。

" OK! OK! 完全明白。我八月三日早上八点半一定会报到"。

感恩我的默想，第一份全职工作，在三个星期后就应允了。实在太好了。我毕身难忘这一位只在短短三十分钟的面试后，肯定我，器重我的领导。沒有他，我的事业身涯可能完全不同。当初，公司也是刚成立，也在组织团队。

从此以后，我在公司和相关企业服务了近二十年，都没有看到公司招聘留台的毕业新生。即便是有相关工作经验的留台生，也是凤毛麟角。

一年一国家

自从全职工作后，我就默想并给自己订下"一年一国家"的旅游计划，也就是说，每一年，一定要到访一个新的国家，反正旧地重遊不计，一定要新的国家。

就这样，1999 年，我有幸被公司选为四十人一团的建厂精英种子队，到日本受训。所以，周一到周五，用功接受培训，周末就是乘坐当时世上数一数二快速的"弹头火车"。遊了东京迪士尼乐园，也遊了银座，名古屋，大板等等。最得意莫过于住宿都是公司负责，还有培训津贴。真的感恩。因为这样，周末才有经济能力到处走马看花，吃喝玩乐。

2000 年，我从日本培训回来，公司建厂完毕并交接给我司，所以大家工作忙得不可开交，很多规范和整改要完善。所以，这一年，就实现了当初答应大学同学，两年后要回台给大家拍照留念，祝贺大家硕士毕业。嗯！我把"台湾"当成自己正式上班后，第一次到访的"一年一国家"计划中的第一站。

2001 年，去了纽西兰环岛。主要是中学知己去了纽西兰留学之后，就留下来工作，成家立业了。她结婚大喜日子，我不但未凑足旅游费，时间点也遇上公司建厂最忙的旱季。所以，在圣诞前夕，年终假期多，工作进度慢等综合考量才出发。与此同时，也是去探访自七十年代出国留学后，在纽西兰落地生根的叔叔一家人。

2002 年是我人生一大重要的里程碑。因为五月第一次"拍拖"的情人，当年的圣诞前夕就注册结婚，变成我相公了。朋友圈还以为咱们是不是"先上车，后补票"？怎么如此匆忙结婚？还是恨嫁？或者可怜没人爱？都不是，真的是一见钟情，彼此也老成熟了。其实我也默想女大三十一定要嫁人。所以眼看自己快要超过适婚年龄了，或说再过几年就是高龄产妇了。另一个最主要因素是他家人催婚了，似乎不娶，我就会落跑。

因为还是情人的老公又瘦又高佻，为了实现"一年一国家"的旅游计划，又要筹备婚礼，所以只能省省消费，选了新加坡上船的四天三夜，买一送一的邮轮配套，又可以一天无限量吃六餐，他又可增肥拍美美婚纱照，我又可实现旅游计划，这应该是最物超所值的选择了吧！

哈哈！未来相公果然成功增胖了六公斤。唯一美中不足是配套是最经济实惠的，所以邮轮睡舱是没有窗户的。我平时又有晕车晕船的缺陷，这样就造成偶尔有晕眩的不舒适感。所以，总往外逛和玩乐，搞到累垮了，就回去倒头就睡，一觉到天明不晕眩。

2003年1月是我摆喜酒，宴请亲朋戚友的美好回忆，正式举行敬茶仪式，过门当人家媳妇儿。所以，我2003年的"一年一国家"旅游计划，刻意提前至2002年12月，到中东的阿曼酋国，并路经迪拜，这主要是公干但也算是计划中，毕竟是新的国家。

2004 年，没来得及计划 "一年一国家" 旅游就怀
第一胎了。当时害喜得乱七八糟，前两个月，几
乎每天请半天病假。由于是第一胎，特别谨慎，
所以都不敢搭乘飞机，轮船等，就乖乖安胎，等
待生产。

2005 年一月分，在惊动医院产房护士医生们之
后，老大以迅雷不及掩耳的速度呱呱坠地。当时
我的羊水破了，冲到医院时才清晨六时，护士己
经看到婴儿头部露出来了。但我清楚记得护士
说："不可用力了，不要大力吸气呼气了。医生
还沒到。不可以生"。

"头都看到了，还不可以生，快点叫医生过来呀
!!。。"我是阵痛到失控了。

"新手妈妈，千万不可以用力。因为你现在才
35.5 周，按医院接生规则，我们必须等妇产科和
小儿科医生到现场，才可以接生，否则任何后果

自负"。护士说道。

感恩两位医生行动敏捷，20 分钟内先后到场。

一吐气一剪用力推，就顺产了。医生剪了脐带，拍一拍婴儿，就听到"哇哇大哭"声了。

"妈妈目前一切身体状况正常"。负责接生的的妇产科医生，待胎盘顺利被排出和完成缝合动作后说道。

"婴儿检查也一切正常。"小儿科医生接着说道，并把小孩往我身上轻轻一放。

在一旁的外子，自小怕血的他已经脸青唇白，双脚冰冷了，感恩在还没吓昏之前就被婴儿哇哇大哭声给唤醒。这种第一次当新手爸妈的感觉，真正毕生难忘的喜悦。

满月后，趁还有产假，我和外子就去一趟巴厘岛，完成 "一年一国家"之旅游计划。也是给自己当新手爸妈的奖励和鼓励。

2006 年，老大周岁，我们决定只去附近的油田国-汶莱。除了完成"一年一国家"旅游计划之外，也让尊敬的姨婆看看孙辈侄女。我的姨姨嫁到汶莱多年，这也是我第一次到访，感恩姨姨依然健谈，始终谦卑敬畏耶和华，她也常常和我传福音。

2007 年，是我人生转捩点。这一年，不想去哪个新国家，只想征服东南亚第一高峰，四千米高的京那岩鲁山，俗称"神山"。谢谢老公兼苦力，为我节省了马币六十令吉的背包代客扛费，所以，老公就是最佳人选了。当然另一个原因是这一组人全是男的，所以，老公又有了另一个重担和角色，也就是私人保镖，幸福如我。

2008 年我思念侨大先修班的香港室友，当时她也是谦卑的基督徒，也常向我传福音。毕业了这么多年，我在这人生转捩点遇见上帝，在主里重生了。我非常想念她，也因为她结婚了多年，我都没当面祝贺。这一年，我来了，我更要把我信主的好消息亲口给她分享。

这一趟，我们先到澳门，乘船去香港，再搭火车去广州，最后又回到澳门。香港点心，澳门葡蛋挞，到今天还是齿间留香，回味无穷。

2009 年，老大快五岁了，我们感谢亚洲廉价航空当时新推出澳洲航线，所以我半夜守在电脑前，凌晨一到就零价机票。哇！抢到了，也当成我们迟来的结婚五周年纪念遊吧！当然也顺道探访中学知己，当时他去了澳洲留学后，领了当地居留证，就一直在澳洲发展置产。另一方面，也希望放松心情，准备怀第二胎了。

感恩上帝的蒙福，回来不久之后就怀孕了。

2010 年，老二刚满月，我也在新的外企公司上班，也是建厂首批员工，当初我负责安排八十员工，包括我自己到美国受训。一伙人周一到周五用功学习，周末就是快乐时光了。我周日早上一定去附近教会参加主日聚会。也在那里认识了很多主里的弟兄姐妹，还一起去吃午饭和参观圣路易斯拱门附近的国家公园，让我人在异乡也感受到主里的爱，无处不在。

2011 年，公司建厂，忙进口和处理不完的的人事招聘与培训，但我也在最忙的时刻怀上第三胎，这时真的是高龄产妇，害喜盛况比前两胎更壮观，但主里内心无限平安和喜乐。

2012 年，顺利产下第三胎后，依然趁产假去了柬埔寨一趟，补齐之前一年的旅游计划。安哥窟和法国面包是最回味的。

2012 年底，我们也去了韩国一趟，当成结婚十周年纪念旅行，也实现一个梦想已久的"冬季恋歌"拍攝场景——南怡岛。在韩国充分享受当地的的交通便捷，市容干净又美观。特别是那碗冬季里暖暖的人参鸡汤，到现在还让我们夫妻俩津津乐道。

这时候的我，开始为"一年一国家"这维持了好多年的旅游计划来献上祷告,但聖灵似乎触动了我的心。。

"是时候放下这个一年一新国家的个人旅游计划了"。

"是时候考虑全家遊，只要是上帝供应的全家快乐遊，那里都开心，不一定要新的国家或新的旅游景点"。

所以，从 2013 年开始，我就听从圣灵的旨意，不再坚持一年旅游一个新国家的个人计划。那一年，我与老公重游台湾，参加大学毕业十五周年聚餐，这也是我老公第一次到访台湾，所以这种成全别人"一年旅游一个新国家"的计划，比成全自己个人更喜悦，此行也顺道去台南探访之前工作的直属领导。

2014 年，我们举家重游汶莱，即便旧地重游也是幸福满满，让姨姨见见老二，且返回美里多住几天，与小孩的大姑一家人联络感情。想想也是第一次到访美里市，非常愧疚，但是迟来好过没来。

2015 年，一家五口在有限的预算之下，买到去台湾的廉价机票，想想台湾之旅是小孩的第一次，又可以和我姐姐一家人相聚，吃吃大学生涯怀念的香鸡排和台湾著名的珍珠奶茶，还有逛不完的夜市，这种旧地重游的喜悦也绝对非笔墨所能形容。

2016 年，感谢上帝的眷顾，让我抢到越南的廉价机票，就这样与爱人去了五天四夜。间中还搭了近 33 小时的火车，从河内到胡志明市。除了下龙湾，号称世界遗址必遊之景点，我们也去了令人揪心的越南战争展示馆。

印象最深刻的还是在市区遇上暴风雨和大淹水，导致巴士一直绕道而行，迟迟未到酒店。更忘不了市区不间断的车子鸣笛声，也见证超过九成的妇女出外工作的勤奋和文化差异，以及越南在东盟十大国家中崛起，后来者居上的魄力。

2017 年，再次感谢上帝透过亚洲航空的供应，我不只三更半夜抢到马尔代夫廉价机票，小姑更协助我们订到超级优惠的水上酒店，真是我俩结婚十五周年纪念的最超值喜乐。因为往外一跳，就是又暖又清晰见底的海水，那种被一群小鱼围绕的幸福，真是美如画。还有踩单车环岛，吹着海风，还有脚踩在雪白的细沙，看日出和日落，在海边吃海鲜大餐等等都是心存无限的感恩，也为彼此维持了十五年的婚姻幸福指数大大加分。

2018 年，因为鼓励了主里姐妹去台湾留学，并承诺在她求学期间一定去探访她。眼看她就要毕业了，一定要一家五口去台湾高雄给她祝贺。就这样，我们又买到廉价的机票，就出发了。去了义守乐园玩了一整天，真的值回票价。看到小孩无数次排队重玩同一个遊乐设施，也别有一番乐趣，仿佛回到童年无知的我，甜蜜有趣。

2019 年，我们一家五口，又买到廉价机票，带小孩出发前往柔佛新山的乐高乐园。我们去了水上乐园，再一次看到小孩们打赤脚，跳跃在无数热烘烘的台阶，重复的排队等待同一个遊乐设施，我由衷感谢上帝的祝福和保守。

和奶奶同房

虽然我因很执著于个人的"一年一国家"旅游计划而努力工作，拼命存钱，但平时的生活一般。我争取与百病缠身的奶奶同房，因为之前错过第一时间发现爷爷中风在床，口吐白沫而起不来又求救不了，我自责很多年。现在，感恩奶奶等到我大学毕业，学成归来，所以我唯一能报答的，就是陪奶奶同房睡觉。

另一个因素，也是父母在楼上主人房，楼下就只有奶奶一个人住，之前家里的姑姑，姐姐都嫁人了，弟弟也出国深造，所以毛遂自荐，晚上同房不同床睡觉，多少有些照应。

除了周一到周五平凡的上班族生活，周六和周日就是奶奶与我的快乐时光。因为我是她车夫，她只管给我行程表。我们常去的地方莫过于诊所或医院之例常身体检查，菜市场，小商店，奶奶老朋友或亲戚的家等等。

当时我开了一辆 600c.c.的小灵鹿，是姐姐嫁到台湾后留下来的。可是身居婆罗洲，布满热带雨林的古晋市，年雨量约 2,500 毫米，加上基础设施还在发展中，所以路上常淹水。

后来考虑自己也喜欢吉普车，比较高和宽，也许较方便载奶奶。就这样，日本培训回来之后，我就买了自己第一辆吉普车，日本二手翻新进口，蓝色车。

开始时，奶奶还有力气抬起脚，踩上车。到后期，奶奶身体太虚弱了，每月都要到医院输血时，我只能用爸爸的国产车载送奶奶。

奶奶与爷爷的性格态度，简直就是天渊之别。爷爷外向爱交谈，奶奶内向话不多。爷爷急躁善于表达情绪，奶奶沉稳有事往心里放。

所以，奶奶即便百病缠身，她也不吭一声，我"百忍成金"的行为特征，或许就是继承了奶奶的良妇品德。

犹记得，有一次在医院输血时，奶奶突然全身抽搐，一反常态。经过证实，是院方疏忽，输入不相容血型的血。

感恩命是保住了，但奶奶的健康，似乎每况愈下。

纽西兰永远的痛

"嬷，今年的聖诞和跨年，我要去纽西兰了。会去找小叔一家人，也会去找我刚嫁人的闺蜜。" 我是用潮州话和奶奶交谈的。

"很好呀！小妹。我这准备了个大红包给你顺风"。奶奶的爱，尽在不言中。

"嬷，你要照顾自己，等我回来，华人新年，我再包个大红包给你，不可以拿你这么多錢啦！" 小妹是我乳名。

我 2001-2002 "一年一国家"旅游跨年计划如期进行。先到北岛，在小叔家住几天，再与闺蜜加入当地的旅游团，出发到南岛。

来到令人陶醉的皇后镇，忽然接到小叔的来电。

"真，我要先回古晋了。你阿嬷应该不行了！"电话另一端传来震惊的消息。

"哇！"我情不自禁，放声大哭，许久说不出话来。

"怎么办？我。。我来问。。。问导游可以。。可以。。开路让我。。我跟你回吗？"我视觉模糊，泪盈满眶，因情绪思维全混乱，许久无法好好说话。

"导游先生，我求求你，可以帮我问问如何回到北岛奥克兰吗？"我哭着哀求导游。

由于我们是订了经济配套，一小车含司机共 12 个人，导游兼司机，会讲中文的。他开了一整天的车已经累垮了。那个时候也到了傍晚了，旅行社不只关门，所有商店营业都几乎关门迎圣诞和新年了。导游得不到他旅行社的帮忙，又不熟悉南岛在这时刻如何买票让我一个人回到北岛。我也不敢三更半夜，人生地不熟，大胆乱跳，且这也是行程的最后第二天。

结果，为了不影响其他同游的好心情。我只能压抑自己无助的情绪默默跟队，心中默想奶奶要等我，我还欠您一个大红包，怎么可以沒见到最后一面就离开呢？

小叔不能等我，独自去机场等待后备机位，随时赶回古晋。所幸其中一趟航班有旅客未到，小叔能及时回到古晋，见奶奶最后一面。

南岛回北产岛的路上，小叔又来电话了。

"小妹，阿嫲过世了。出殡日是一月二日，你来得及参加。"。妈用小叔电话给我传来噩耗。

"哇！我一月一日晚上到，二号就出殡？"我边说边痛哭，久久不能自已。

沒想到，出发前的一席话，原来是与奶奶最后的话别。原来奶奶心里有数，但她本性含蓄，就是不说出口，还祝福我。

跟奶奶同房，最终还是无法在她临终前陪她走完人生旅程。

纽西兰之旅，我永远的痛。

隐形的爱之前奏曲

我三十三岁，也就是 2007 年中到 2008 年初，是人生的转捩点.

自从 1998 年留台归来，除了埋头苦干，努力实现个人"一年一国家"旅游计划之外，就是顺理成章的结婚，生小孩，买房买车等。

照理说，这么吉祥如意又丰富的生活，似乎是大家追求的梦想生活，应该是大部份人羡慕的小家庭生活，说真的沒什么好埋怨了。

可是我在物质上无所缺之当下，发现自己心灵就是空虚，就是不踏实。想起自有记忆以来，我每件事都喜欢默想，往往默想之后，内心一股暖流，一股冲劲，勇往直前就成事了，心中充满爱与无限感恩。

我三十三岁这一年，这一股隐形的力量，越来越强烈，似乎要把我带到祂面前。

"真，我刚去上了第一课的《信心满满做父母》，很棒也，下一堂课，你要不要跟我一起去？"我那纽西兰的闺蜜，带着女儿回来古晋上一年的幼稚园，刚好遇上这个课程。

"好呀！，我也正寻找类似的课程，因为我家老大也快上幼稚园了，我们一定要掌握做父母的技巧，走在小孩的前面，引导他们，带领他们走对的路"。我犹如发现新大陆，兴奋无比。

就这样，我与闺蜜一起上第二堂课，至到完成整个课程，还去了讲师家参加了结业聚餐。

在上课时，偶尔听到课程召集人以"牧师"称呼讲师。当时的我，真不知道"牧师"是什么意思。也没感兴趣去寻问或进一步探讨。

但是，这股奇妙隐形的爱，在讲师结业聚餐里又涌上心头了。我问道：

"我每次遇到困难或有所求时，就会默想，这股隐形的奇妙力量，让我发自内心的平安又有动力，请问为什么会这样？"

"这是你给天父的祷告。创造你的天父，当你还在母体里，祂就认识你，就爱你了。这股隐形的爱，就是上帝奇妙无私的爱"。讲师解释道。

与此同时，讲师请他内人在房里拿出一小册子，递给我。
"这册子，你带回去用心，好好的读，若那股隐形的爱感动你读完最后这段话，我们再进一步认识上帝这奇妙隐形的爱，好吗？"讲师清楚的解释道。

"好的!好的!我读完再找讲师。谢谢。"我答应著。

那天晚上，我读了又读，有读但不是很懂。但是最后这段话，我是用心，全心全意的读了好几篇，也不是很懂。但这股隐形的爱，瞬间把我平时的担忧给带走，瞬间把我内心的空虚填满，笔墨无法形容的平安和喜乐。

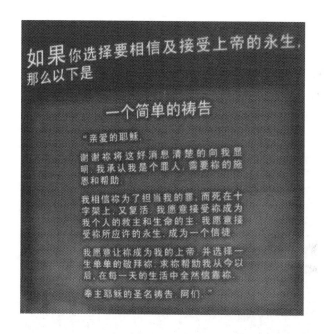

如果你选择要相信及接受上帝的永生，那么以下是

一个简单的祷告

"亲爱的耶稣，

谢谢祢将这好消息清楚的向我显明，我承认我是个罪人，需要祢的施恩和帮助。

我相信祢为了担当我的罪，而死在十字架上，又复活，我愿意接受祢成为我个人的救主和生命的主，我愿意接受祢所应许的永生，成为一个信徒。

我愿意让祢成为我的上帝，并选择一生单单的敬拜祢，求祢帮助我从今以后，在每一天的生活中全然信靠祢。

奉主耶稣的圣名祷告，阿们。"

"讲师，我已经读完你给我的册子。尤其最后这段话，我读了又读，请问接下来，我要怎么做？还要读那些材料？"我见到讲师时，迫不及待的追问这股隐形的爱所带来的平安和喜乐。

"恭喜你选择了耶稣作为你的主，接受主耶稣成为你的救主。这奇妙隐形的爱也是上帝的恩典，因为祂无私的爱，上帝把祂唯一的独生子耶稣，在两千多年前，为了赦免你和我的罪，被钉在十字架上，祂的宝血把你和我的罪洗净，救赎了我们。耶稣第三天复活，象征着信祂的，我们的灵命就得到重生了"。

"接下来，我希望你继续认识这位奇妙，拥有无私的爱的上帝，我会安排主里的姐妹进一步给你分享《我们的基督徒生命》,好吗？"讲师说道。

"好的!好的!对了，讲师，为什么嘉妮女士称呼您牧师？请问，牧师是什么意思？"我无知的问道，一个在我脑里超过半年的疑问。

"我在教会全职侍奉，就像牧羊人带领一群羔羊，我也教导我的羊读聖经，了解上帝的话语，与祂建立关系。所以，牧羊人加导师，就简称牧师了。你就是我其中一只失散多年，寻找许久的羊，感谢主，赞美主。你的救恩得着了"。牧师耐心回应。
"呀。。。牧师好，谢谢牧师。。我。。我一定会努力。。努力认识这位救主。"我很感激，但话里也道出千万个问号。什么牧羊人，什么羊，什么救恩，什么赦免，救赎，重生。。。

"真真，再次恭喜你，我们继续在主里成长，上帝的爱是隐形的爱，但也是真真实实无私的爱，有信心，有盼望。结束之前，我和师母可以为你做个祷告吗？"牧师问。

"好的!好的!"我期待这个新体验。

"亲爱的天父，感谢祢把真真带到我们的《信心满满做父母》课程，感谢祢的恩典，真真接受祢成为她的救主。主啊！感谢真真如此渴慕祢，追求祢从小对真真隐形的爱。主啊！我们把真真交付于祢的恩手当中，求主继续带领她，保守她和家人。主啊！我们也祷告祢让真真充满主的智慧，与主里姐妹配合，努力完成《我们的基督徒生命》的学习，时时刻刻与祢建立关系，读圣经。主啊！我们再次为真真的救恩献上感恩，为她的得着而无限喜悦，我们把这一切的荣耀归于主，以上所求，是奉主耶稣的圣名求，阿们"。

牧师很长的祷告。

"谢谢!"那个时候的我，还不知道应该回应"阿们"。

那是 2007 年底，我真心接着这股自幼深藏在我内心隐形的爱，这位拥有奇妙无私的爱的耶稣基督为我的救主。从此，我每一天的生命，都是活得有信心，有盼望。有困难，信靠祂不懼怕，有成就，荣耀归于主。

信主之后，圣经里的一个人物，先知耶利米，尤其在耶利米书第一章第五节记载到「*我未將你造在腹中，我已曉得你；你未出母胎，我已分別你為聖；我已派你作列國的先知。*」这句经文给了我很大的触动。

上帝對於今日的每一個人也都安排了計畫,就像祂早已对先知耶利米有安排，有计划。

回想自己自有记忆以来，虽然不曾真正认识耶稣，也没接受祂为救主，更不会凡事信靠祂，但祂一直在我成长人生旅途中，引导我到祂所指定的特殊位置。而要找到自己的特殊位置，我就必须有能力，努力地實行上帝對於我的旨意和計畫。这取決於我全然顺服和跟随祂的能力和決心。

当时有求必应的默想，其实就是这股能力，因为应允了上帝安排给我的旨意和計畫，再加上努力行动，就成事。

后来，神的话语再次透过圣经诗篇 139，第 13 节到十六节，肯定我这股自小默想的能力，其实就是上帝预备给我的命定。

「*我的肺腑是祢所造的，我在母腹中，祢已覆庇我。我要稱謝祢，因我受造奇妙可畏；祢的作為奇妙，這是我心深知道的。我在暗中受造，在地的深處被聯絡，那時我的形體並不向祢隱藏。我未成形的體質，祢的眼早已看見了；祢所定的日子，我尚未度一日，祢都寫在祢的冊上了。*」

信主之后的新生命，有太多太多的见证。。。
（待续）